Written In Honor and Gratitude to

The Immaculate Heart of Mary

For all of her prayers for sinners like me

"But Mary kept all these things,
pondering them in her heart."(Lk.2:19)

"...and a sword will pierce through your heart." (Lk.2:35)

"...his mother kept all these things in her heart." (Lk.2:51)

The
ROSARY
is the
ANSWER

Father Herbert Burke

Queenship

PUBLISHING COMPANY
P.O. Box 220 • Goleta, CA 93116
(800) 647-9882 • (805) 692-0043 • Fax: (805) 967-5133
www.queenship.org

Library of Congress Number # 2006930584

Published by:
> Queenship Publishing
> P.O. Box 220
> Goleta, CA 93116
> (800) 647-9882 • (805) 692-0043 • Fax: (805) 967-5133
> www.queenship.org

Printed in the United States of America

ISBN: 1-57918-309-3

Table of Contents

Chapter 1

The Rosary is the Answer

"And a great portent appeared in heaven, a woman clothed with the sun, with the moon under her feet, and on her head a crown of twelve stars...Then the dragon was angry with the woman, and went off to make war on the rest of her offspring, on those who keep the commandments of God and bear testimony to Jesus." (Rev.12:1,17)

Why Pray the Rosary?

Prayer is the stairway to heaven, and the Rosary is the prayer from heaven. The prayer of the Rosary is the Word of God in action, and the action is conquering sin and returning to God.

The word *Rosary* means "A Crown of Roses." The Rosary makes a spiritual garden in our soul of the fruits of the Holy Spirit (Gal.5:22-24), and the flowers of virtue. When you pray the Rosary devoutly you are making a spiritual crown which scripture calls a *"never fading crown of glory."* (1Pt.5:4) You make one for yourself, and a crown of spiritual Roses for Our Lady. These prayers produce heavenly Roses which remind her of the joy of the Annunciation (Lk.1:28), and are united to the *Crown of Glory* (1Pt.5:4) given her by the Holy Trinity when they placed *on her head a crown of twelve stars* (Rev.12:1) and crowned her Queen of Heaven. The Rosary is *the Psalter of Jesus and Mary*, the first sacred words of the Gospel commanded by God the Father, and delivered to Mary by the Archangel Gabriel (Lk.1:28). The Rosary is a great spiritual weapon, it is the sword of the Christian soldier, it is the *"word of God... living and active, sharper than any two-edged sword"* (Heb.4:12). It is the Word of God in prayer and the Gospel in meditation, it is the answer to the spiritual enemies of man. The Rosary is the word of God in action—destroying vice and bringing grace within our soul. Scripture speaks of our spiritual warfare within as being more important than any external physical warfare.

"Finally, be strong in the Lord and in the strength of his might. Put on the whole armor of God, that you may be able to stand against the wiles of the devil. For we are not contending against flesh and blood, but against the principalities, against the powers, against the world rulers of this present darkness, against the spiritual hosts of wickedness... And take the helmet of salvation, and the sword of the Spirit, which is the word of God. Pray at all times in the Spirit with all prayer and supplication." (Eph. 6:10-18)

Many Catholics who have been imprisoned or persecuted for their faith throughout the centuries and even today, have kept their courage, their sanity, and their souls through the Rosary. Pope John Paul II said:

"The Rosary is my favourite prayer...To recite the Rosary is nothing other than to contemplate with Mary the face of Christ." (Apostolic Letter Rosarium Virginis Mariae, Copyright Libreria Editrice Vaticana)

The Rosary is the primary devotion to Mary. The Rosary is a Christ-centered, biblical prayer which combines meditation on the life of Jesus and Mary with the Lord's prayer and the Hail Mary.

The Rosary is the weapon of the spiritual and the physical soldier. Although the Rosary is a spiritual weapon, its feast day October 7th was founded on a military victory by the Christian forces of Europe against an attacking Turkish Armada. The Pope called on the people of Europe and the Christian Military, which was greatly outnumbered, to pray the Rosary for victory over the attacking Moslem Turkish invaders. Through the intervention of these prayers, the small Christian fleet routed the physically superior Turkish Fleet. If the Rosary can stop an attacking armada, consider how powerful it can be for your spiritual life! St. Padre Pio used to simply call his rosary, "The Weapon". He said, "The Holy Rosary is the weapon for all who want to win every battle." It is the Spiritual Light Sabre for the Knights of God, as St. Paul says, *"Let us then cast off the works of darkness and put on the armor of light."* (Rom.13:12).

The Story of Our Lady at Fatima

The Story of Fatima is a truly wonderful story of Our Lady's love for us. She came with a message and a miracle. The miracle she worked was called the Miracle of the Sun. On that day, October 13, 1917, over 50,000 people, those in the immediate area, and many far away, witnessed the Sun spin and head for the earth. Many cried out for mercy and forgiveness thinking it was the end of the world. However, the Sun returned to its natural place in the sky, and the proof that Our Lady was indeed appearing to these three little children in Fatima Portugal, 1917 was given beyond a doubt. Needless to say, the Chapel to Our Lady was built, and thousands converted from sinful lives and even from atheism on that great day that the miracle promised on October 13th was fulfilled.

Although she came several times and said other things, here I only quote a bit from the first and the sixth Apparitions to give the reader a sense of the main message. First here is the message:

The First and Sixth Apparitions of Our Lady at Fatima

The First Apparition of Our Lady at Fatima

We had only gone a few steps further when, there before us on a small holmoak, we beheld a Lady all dressed in white. She was more brilliant than a crystal glass filled with sparkling water, when the rays of the burning sun shine through it.

We stopped, astounded, before the apparition. We were so close, just a few feet from her, that we were bathed in the light which surrounded her, or rather, which radiated from her.

Then Our Lady spoke to us:

"Do not be afraid. I will do you no harm."

"Where are you from?"

"I am from heaven."

"I have come to ask you to come here for six months in succession, on the 13th day, at this same hour. Later on, I will tell you who I am and what I want. Afterwards, I will return here yet a seventh time."

"Shall I go to heaven too?"

"Yes, you will."

"And Jacinta?"

"And Francisco?"

"He will go there too, but he must say many Rosaries."

Then I remembered to ask about two girls who had died recently. They were friends of mine and used to come to my home to learn weaving with my eldest sister.

"Is Maria das Neves in heaven?"

"Yes, she is."(I think she was about 16 years old).

"And Amelia?"

"She will be in purgatory until the end of the world." (It seems to me that she was between 18 and 20 years of age.)

"Are you willing to offer yourselves to God and bear all the suffering He wills to send you, as an act of reparation for the sins by which He is offended, and of supplication for the conversion of sinners?"

"Yes, we are willing."

"Then you are going to have much to suffer, but the grace of God will be your comfort."

... "Pray the Rosary every day, in order to obtain peace for the world, and the end of the war." [WWI]

The Sixth Apparition of Our Lady at Fatima

"I want to tell you that a chapel is to be built here in my honor. I am the Lady of the Rosary. Continue always to pray the Rosary every day. The war is going to end, and the soldiers will soon return to their homes."

I have many things to ask you: the cure of some sick persons, the conversion of sinners, and other things..."

"Some yes, but not others. They must amend their lives and ask forgiveness for their sins."

Looking very sad, Our Lady said:

"Do not offend the Lord our God any more, because He is already so much offended."

(*The Message of Fatima*, Lucia Speaks, AMI Press, Washington NJ. 1997 Revised Ed. pgs.9, 11-13, 29)

Jacinta and Francisco both died a few years later, and Lucia joined the Carmelite Sisters as a Nun. Sister Lucia was one of the three children Mary appeared to at Fatima. She said:

"The Most Holy Virgin, in these last times in which we live, has given a new efficacy to the recitation of the Rosary, to such an extent, that there is no problem, no matter how difficult it is, temporal or especially spiritual, in the personal life of each one of us, of our families, of the families of the world or of the religious communities or even of the life of peoples and nation, that cannot be solved by the Rosary. There is no problem I tell you, no matter how difficult it is, that we cannot solve by the prayer of the Holy Rosary. With the Holy Rosary, we will save ourselves. We will sanctify ourselves. We will console our Lord and obtain the salvation of many souls."(Sister Lucia of Fatima to Father Fuentes, Interview on December 26, 1957)

In other words, whatever your problems are - the Rosary is the Answer.

The Witness of Blessed Mother Teresa of Calcutta

Blessed Mother Teresa of Calcutta writes how the combination of Eucharistic Adoration and the Rosary blessed her community with more vocations:

"I make a Holy hour each day in the presence of Jesus in the Blessed Sacrament. All my sisters of the Missionaries of Charity make a daily holy hour, as well, because we find that through our daily holy hour our love for Jesus becomes more intimate, our love for each other more understanding, and our love for the poor more compassionate. Our holy hour is our daily family prayer where we get together and pray the Rosary before the exposed Blessed Sacrament the first half hour, and the second half hour we pray in silence. Our adoration has doubled the number of our vocations. In 1963 we were making a weekly holy hour together, but it was not until 1973, when we began our daily holy hour that our community started to grow and blossom." (Rosary Meditations from Mother Teresa of Calcutta, Loving Jesus with the Heart of Mary, Eucharistic Meditations on the Fifteen Mysteries of the Rosary, pg.3, Copyright, Missionaries of the Blessed Sacrament, Plattsburgh, N.Y.)

In the parish where I am pastor, we have begun Eucharistic Exposition with the Rosary before our Sunday Masses. Our Lord said, *"...and I, when I am lifted up from the earth, will draw all men to myself."* (Jn.12:32), and since we have lifted him up on the altar in the Monstrance he has done just that. Many people are now coming up to an hour earlier before mass to join in Eucharistic Adoration and the Rosary before Mass. And, the number of converts has increased since we have started this practice. Many people are unable to get to the holy hour offered during the week, so I have arranged it so they can combine Eucharistic Adoration, the Rosary, and Holy Mass on Sunday. It is wonderful to see a church full of people praying the rosary and adoring the Eucharist in preparation for Mass.

Ultimately, sin is the cause of every problem and prayer is the solution. Sin is the stairway to hell, and prayer is the stairway to heaven. Whatever problems we can't trace back to sins we have committed, we can trace back to those others have committed, including original sin (Gen.3 16-19,Rom.8:19-22). Sin separates us from God, prayer reunites us to God. Prayer is lifting our hearts and minds to God. Ven. Louis of Granada says: "Prayer is a royal gate through which the soul enters into the heart of God; a foretaste of the glory to come." (*Summa of the Christian Life*, Translated by Fr. Jordan Aumann,O.P., Copyright 1979, TAN Books and Publishers, Inc. Rockford, Il.) St. Augustine says: "Prayer is the key of Heaven.... As our body cannot live without nourishment, so our soul cannot spiritually be kept alive without prayer." St. Alphonsus says: "He who prays, is saved; he who prays not, is damned!"

The main goal of the devil is to keep us from prayer. We often find we have no time for God, but plenty of time for the world. We aren't so motivated to pray, but we are often motivated to sin. If we learn the value of prayer, and the horror of sin, we can overcome the daily temptation not to pray.

The World War I Story

The late Archbishop Fulton J. Sheen, Servant of God, once wrote about the power of the Rosary. In his book *"The World's First Love"* (copyright 1952, Fulton J.Sheen, Published by McGraw-Hill Book Company, Inc. N.Y., Reprinted 1996 by Ignatius Press, San Francisco, pgs. 214, 215) he wrote:

The power of the Rosary is beyond description. And here I am reciting concrete instances, which I know. Young people, in danger of death through accident, have had miraculous recoveries; a mother, despaired of in childbirth, was saved with the child; alcoholics became temperate; dissolute lives became spiritualized; fallen-aways returned to the Faith; the childless were blessed with a family; soldiers were preserved during battle; mental anxieties were overcome; and pagans were converted. I know of a Jew who, in World War I, was in a shell hole on the Western Front with four Austrian soldiers. Shells had been bursting on all sides.

Suddenly, one shell killed his four companions. He took the beads from the hands of one of them and began to say the Rosary. He knew it by heart, for he had heard others say it so often. At the end of the first decade, he felt an inner warning to leave that shell hole. He crawled through much mud and muck and threw himself into another. At that moment a shell hit the first hole, where he had been lying. Four more times, exactly the same experience; four more warnings, and four times his life was saved! He promised then to give his life to Our Lord and to His Blessed Mother if he should be saved. After the war more sufferings came to him; his family was burned by Hitler, but his promise lingered on. Recently, I baptized him—and the grateful soldier is now preparing to study for the priesthood.

Ultimately why do we pray? We pray so that we can go to heaven. Scripture says prayer is powerful: *"Those who trust in you cannot be put to shame."* (Dan.3:40) *"The unceasing prayer of a just man is of great avail."* (Jam.5:16-18) Scripture shows how prayer can change things, and certain things will only happen *if* we pray:

In those days Hezekiah became sick and was at the point of death. And Isaiah the prophet...came to him, and said to him, "Thus says the Lord, 'Set your house in order; for you shall die, you shall not recover.'" Then Hezekiah turned his face to the wall, and prayed to the Lord, saying "Remember now, O Lord, I beseech thee, how I have walked before thee in faithfulness and with a whole heart, and have done what is good in thy sight." And Hezekiah wept bitterly. And before Isaiah had gone out of the middle court, the word of the Lord came to him: "Turn back, and say to Hezekiah the prince of my people, Thus says the Lord, the God of David your father: I have heard your prayer, I have seen your tears; behold, I will heal you; on the third day you shall go up to the house of the Lord. And I will add fifteen years to your life. I will deliver you and this city out of the hand of the king of Assyria, and I will defend this city for my own sake and for my servant David's sake." (2 Kings 20:1-6), (Joshua 10:12-14, Daniel 6).

The World War II Story

A great example of the powerful protection that comes from Mary through the rosary is given in this war and rosary story which comes from the Second World War:

My friend Don Ruff was a tail gunner in the Army Air Corps during WWII. His bomber crew consisted of 11 personnel. While flying on a mission over the China Sea, Don was praying his rosary, as was his custom. He was positioned after the bomb bay that held nine 500-pound bombs. Something triggered an explosion and Don's next recollection was coming to, 30 feet under the water, praying the Hail Mary.

The plane had been flying at 5,000 feet when the explosion occurred and plummeted a mile to the sea. Don remembers seeing wreckage and body parts as he made his way to the surface. The surface of the sea was aflame with burning fuel and he had to splash the surface to keep the flames away. There was always the danger of sharks, but after a short while Don was picked up and brought to shore to the Naval hospital.

They put a screen around Don because he was expected to die. Don fooled them all and came home to eventually marry the fiancee of his buddy who died in the crash. He is now the father of eight and grandfather to numerous children. Don was closest to the explosion, and yet he is the sole survivor from the exploded and crashed bomber. This incident is briefly covered in the military logs. Don Koch, Surprise, Arizona. (*101 Inspirational Stories of the Rosary*, by Sister Patricia Proctor, OSC,Franciscan Monastery of St. Clare, Spokane, WA, Copyright 2003, pg.114)

The Rosary versus the Atom Bomb

Even the Atomic Bomb is not more powerful than the Rosary! One of the most concrete examples of the power of the Rosary came at the end of World War II. On August 6, 1945 the first atomic bomb used in war was dropped on Hiroshima, but the power of Our Lady's Rosary was present to protect the priests of the Church of Our Lady's Assumption. By all logic and physics the four priests in the rectory should have been dead, but by the supernatural power of God and the Rosary, they were still alive! When the bomb exploded half a million people were killed, and the city was vaporized, but the four priests in the rectory were saved! The four Jesuit priests, Fathers Hugo Lassalle, Kleinsorge, Cieslik and Schiffer, opened the door after the blast of the bomb to find there was no more street, and virtually no more city. They could see the hills, which normally were blocked by all the building of the city. They were living the message of Fatima and devoted to the Rosary, and so the Rosary was victorious even over the Atomic Bomb! Oddly enough, in a novena nine days later, on the feast of the Assumption August 15th, peace came and World War II ended.

Another evil of World War II happened when the Allies gave Catholic Austria to the Russian Communists. Since they were hopelessly outnumbered militarily, another solution was sought. A priest named Pater Petrus remembered the victory of Our Lady of the Rosary over the Turkish Military and asked for ten percent of the Austrians to promise to pray the Rosary each day for the Russians to go. After seven years of prayers, in a perplexing footnote in history, the communist pulled out on the anniversary of the Fatima apparitions, May 13,1955. The Rosary is more powerful than an army with machine guns!

In another victory of Our Lady's Rosary we see how prayer fought communism and won. In 1962 the communists were ready to take over Brazil, just like they did in Cuba. Giant protests of thousands of women in Brazil formed praying the Rosary in Sao Paulo. They proclaimed that the nation God gave them was in danger of being enslaved like Cuba, Poland, and Hungary. They called on the Mother of God to save their nation from this fate. With the Rosary and the "Campaign of Women for Democracy", the Communists were stopped. See the 1964 November issue of Reader's Digest, in a story titled, "The Country that Saved Itself."

The Sensual Persecution

In the United States and other nations today we have a persecution that is perhaps even more deadly. We have a persecution not of pain, put of pleasure; not of a dictator's iron fist, but of a playboy's velvet glove. We do not so much fear totalitarian control, but a free licence to almost any sin. What is forbidden is prayer in schools, what is taught is paganism through the new "sex education classes." The integrity of faith in God has been taken out of the fabric of education. As a result the moral character of children fails since they need the guidance of faith to control their lower nature. Instead of prayer we have the police or security guards in many schools, when they were not needed in the 30's, 40's, and 50's.

The norms of decency have been breached. Children's innocence is being destroyed by this sensual persecution. Impure images, immodest dress, vulgar language, is common place in tv commercials, shows, and movies, with no sufficient outrage. A frog in water will remain while we slowly raise the temperature until it boils and he dies, so too, our media and culture has slowly raised the tolerance for sin until we have made the most heinous sins socially acceptable and we are spiritually dying as a society. We have a "sensual persecution" that causes the public culture, especially through wealthy pagans who control the media, to be directed against the 10 commandments. Our lower natures are encouraged and allowed to proceed unchecked in this animalistic environment. The worldly do not understand that excessive sexual sins are the precursors for violence. Sins of weakness lead to sins of malice, and ultimately to sins against the Holy Spirit. Christ prophesied about the end times, *"And because wickedness is multiplied, most men's love will grow cold."* (Mt.24:12) .

A great spiritual battle is occurring in our midst. It is happening at all levels. It is within politics, within churches, within the media, and first and foremost within the heart of each individual who decides for himself to side with God or to follow the world and it's "god". All we have to do is look at the physical external manifestation of this spiritual internal warfare. Our public television is filled with impure images, our justice system is breaking down, our neighborhoods are becoming more dangerous, our children and schools are filled with drugs and alcohol, despair and confusion, suicide, and murder such as the Columbine Massacre. And, as it gets worse, children are having children, and little teens and even pre-teens are having abortions or giving birth when they themselves aren't raised. This is the spilling over of adult irresponsibility into the realm of the child's world. This child's world is supposed to be shielded and protected from this excessive sensuality and animalistic hedonism, but it is not. The result is that the next generation is being raised without any spirituality, has a moral character disadvantage, and then it gets worse for their children.

Scripture foresees the selfish and destructive thoughts of this old pagan mentality being reborn in our modern cultures:

"Come, therefore, let us enjoy the good things that exist, and make use of the creation to the full as in youth. Let us take our fill of costly wine and perfumes... Let none of us fail to share in our revelry, everywhere let us leave signs of enjoyment, because this is our portion, and this our lot. Let us oppress the righteous poor man; let us not spare the widow nor regard the gray hairs of the aged. But let our might be our law of right, for what is weak proves itself to be useless. Let us lie in wait for the righteous man, because he is inconvenient to us and opposes our actions; he reproaches us for sins against the law, and accuses us of sins against our training. He professes to have knowledge of God, and calls himself a child of the Lord. He became to us a reproof of our thoughts; the very sight of him is a burden to us, because his manner of life is unlike that of others, and his ways are strange. We are considered by him as something base, and he avoids our ways as unclean; he calls the last end of the righteous happy, and boasts that God is his father... Thus they reasoned, but they were led astray, for their wickedness blinded them, and they did not know the secret purposes of God, nor hope for the wages of holiness..." (Wis. 2:6-16, 21, 22)

This "sensual persecution" distorts our spiritual values, and blinds us to the truths of God. It is a flood of the senses that must be resisted with prayer, or we will be washed away in its dirty waves. It doesn't matter how much money we make, how many friends we have, how famous we are, or how many pleasures we experience—our life is a failure if we don't make it to heaven. Our Lord said: *"What does it profit a man if he gain the whole world, but lose his own soul?"* (Mt.16:26) *"If any man would come after me, let him deny himself and take up his cross and follow me. For whoever would save his life will lose it, and whoever loses his life for my sake will find it."* (Mt.16:24, 25). We are called to sacrifice the life of sin for the life of grace, the pleasures of the flesh for the joys of the spirit, so that we will gain a new life in heaven. *"How can a young man keep his way pure? By guarding it according to Thy word."* (Ps.119:9). The rosary is the word of God in action, if we are faithful to it, it will help keep us and our children from sin.

Father Peyton's Family Rosary Crusade

The great solution to this evil of society was offered by Father Patrick Peyton. He is one of my personal heroes, and I would have liked to have met him. Unfortunately, he died at 83 on June 3rd 1992, three days before I was ordained. As a young man, in his last year of seminary, Father

Patrick Peyton became ill and was dying of tuberculous. The doctors offered him a choice between a desperate operation that would leave him badly handicapped or to turn to God in prayer for a miracle. Father Cornelius Hagerty counseled the young seminarian on his hospital bed to use the faith he brought with him from Ireland, and to trust in Our Lady's Intercession. He decided against the operation, and he prayed the rosary asking for a cure. He recovered fully and in gratitude to Our Lady of the Rosary, he went on to start "The Family Rosary Crusade." This Rosary crusade went on to fill stadiums and involved prominent movie stars who helped his "Family Theater" productions on radio and television shows, promoting the Family Rosary. St. John Chrysostom said: "God governs the world, but prayer governs God himself!" and St. John Vianney said, "I know something stronger than God: the man who prays. He gets God to say, 'Yes', when He would have said, 'No'." There are three answers to prayer: yes, no, and please wait. There are certain gifts God wishes to give us, which we can only have if we ask for them in prayer. Fr. Peyton was able to get God to cure him through prayer, when he would have died without it!

Father Patrick Peyton said: "If families give Our Lady fifteen minutes a day by reciting the Rosary, I assure them that their homes will become, by God's grace, peaceful places." He sought to bring peace to the world by bringing peace to the family, through prayer. Father Peyton tried to get families to pray 5 decades of the Rosary each day. If this is too intimidating at first, then maybe one decade would be a good way to start. In my homilies I try to get young married couples, and especially ones with children, to pray *at least* one decade a day, together. It only takes five minutes at most to pray 1 decade. In this way they receive the protection and prayers of Our Lady in their families and in their marriages. Prayer will add a divine dimension to their human romance and help them in their marriage.

For those who still find one decade too much of a challenge I have another option. I try to get families who have trouble getting together for prayer to at least pray one Our Father and one Hail Mary, in thanksgiving for their meals. This will take little more than 1 minute. It's hard to find a good excuse not to do that one! By the end of the year they will have completed 365 Our Fathers and 365 Hail Marys. This is equivalent to the prayers in almost 7 rosaries, and it would only take a few seconds before the meal. How easy it is to do, and how great a blessing it would gain for a family.

The Rosary is the Answer

The blessings of the Rosary in families also came to my own family. It was my father who taught me about the Rosary when I was a child, and ironically, I wound up helping my father return to it in his old age. Before his death I had been praying for my father to get back to the rosary since he was getting older and closer to the day he would enter eternity, and he didn't seem to be as prayerful as I thought he could be. He told me about a dream he had in which he saw the Blessed Mother looking at him and holding out a Rosary to him saying: "*This is the Answer.*" After that he returned to the Rosary with more devotion than he had before. Despite the many difficulties he faced in his last days, my Father was prepared at the hour of his death, by the prayers of Our Lady. I had been a priest for only a year when he died. I was able to get home to visit him after the Sunday Masses were done. He seemed unusually interested in the spiritual life that day. He kept talking about spiritual things. I remember he said to me, "The most important thing in life is to love God and keep his commandments; nothing else matters." I was the priest and he was preaching to me! Needless to say I was pleased with his new attitude and have stuck in my mind those last few words he said to me.

I had no idea when I hugged him goodbye and told him that I loved him that it would be the last time I saw him alive. I believe that although neither he nor I knew it would be his last day on earth, Our heavenly Father and Mother knew, and she kept her pledge to him to pray for him at the hour of his death. This is the great beauty of the Hail Mary prayer. Mary not only prays for us when we pray the Rosary, but she prays for us at that last hour, when the devil makes his last chance to tempt our souls away from Christ. Thus, the beauty of the ending of the Hail Mary, "*pray for us sinners now, and at the hour of our death*", was brought home to me so powerfully on the day of my father's death. I saw how he changed so dramatically that last day, and had a great interest in the spiritual life as a result of the prayers of Mary at the hour of his death. I am eternally grateful for my Father and Mother who taught me how to pray the Rosary and showed me by their example the importance of the rosary.

The power of the Rosary and the love of Our Lady for souls is so great! Even if you are neglectful, even after committing big sins, Our Lady of the Rosary will always take you back and again answer your prayers because she is the "Refuge of Sinners." Our Lady loves sinners, she wants to pray for them and make them saints. I am a big sinner, and I need all the help I can get!

I am encouraged by St. Hilary's words written so long ago (368A. D)— "However great a sinner may have been, if he shows himself devout to Mary, he will never perish." (*The Voice of the Saints*, Francis W. Johnston, copyright 1965, Burns & Oates, London, pg.139) When we pray the Rosary, we enable Our Lady to pray for us in a powerful way that she could not do otherwise. The Rosary is the arm of the love of Mary.

My parents met during World War II. My father met my mother at a USO dance. She was a Southern Baptist and a southern belle. Many years after their marriage my mother decided to become a Catholic. I can't say for sure, but I suspect my father prayed the Rosary for her to do so. Once I asked my mother about it and she told me that after going to mass and listening to homilies so long she realized that the Catholic Church didn't teach anything that was against the Bible.

I am grateful for her emphasis on the Bible because when I was a child my mother used to read to me from the Bible almost every night. Even when she didn't read to me, I used to like to look at the pictures. I was fascinated with them, and they told the sacred stories in a way that I could understand even without someone reading them. It can make a great impression on a young child to be alone and looking at the pictures from the Bible. They say a picture is worth a thousand words, and for a little boy who can't read it's really true! It was a wonderful thing for me as a child to have my own Bible. I think that this had a great influence on my faith and my recognition of my vocation. As a child I was not afraid to say I believed in God. I received a good basic understanding of God and a strong faith from this simple encounter with the Children's Bible.

Although this occurred when I was only four and five, I think it left a lifetime impression on me. The famous poem reads: "The child is the father of the man". The way a child is, he shall be as an adult. We learn so much in those first few years of our lives, and our minds are able to learn quicker as children than adults. The most important knowledge we can have is about the One who created us, the One who died for us, the One Whom we shall be closest to in eternity—God. In addition to learning how to talk, learning to love our parents, relatives, friends, learning to love God should be just as important for small children. I am so grateful for the time my mother spent with me, reading to me before I could read, from God's word. Our Lord said: *"Let the children come to me, and do not hinder them; for to such belongs the kingdom of God. Truly, I say to you, whoever does not receive the kingdom of God like a child shall not enter it."* (Lk.18:16,17)

Before I was born my mother had some miscarriages. It was of such great concern to my parents that they prayed the Rosary for God to send them another child, and that everything would be all right with this one. My mother conceived again, but began to get the feeling that she would lose me. The doctor told her to get in bed and stay there. In answer to my parents Rosary I escaped the miscarriage and was born healthy on my mother's birthday, August 22. On the old Church calender this was the feast of the Immaculate Heart of Mary. On the new calender it is the feast of the Queenship of Mary, the last of the Glorious Mysteries of the Rosary. Although they didn't ask for a priest, for a good boy, or a bad boy, I think they got all three! My parents and my family life were not perfect, but we always had love in our family. My priesthood hasn't been perfect, but I have always tried to love the Lord, and seek his forgiveness for my weaknesses. Thus far he has given me the grace and opportunity to persevere and to try to improve and correct any failures.

My parents brought me into the Church as an infant through Baptism shortly after birth. Although this was a decision made for me, it was a decision that I would later embrace fully—but not without a struggle. So too, is the grace of final perseverance, which I hope to yet achieve, not without a struggle (*...and you will be hated by all for my name's sake. But he who endures to the end will be saved. Mt.10:22*). St. Paul says: *"But I chastise my body, and bring it into subjection: lest perhaps, after I have preached to others, I myself should become lost."* (1Cor.9:27)

I remember quite distinctly how the world began to get its clutches around my soul and slowly lead me away from my faith as I went through elementary school. The world worked on me through television, the influence of bad friends and most of all through a total neglect of prayer outside of Sunday Mass.

But help was coming through my spiritual Mother. This came when my father gave me a Miraculous Medal. I was pleased with the medal and intrigued by its design. I asked God to help me get closer to Him. The answer to this prayer came as an inspiration to pray another prayer.

One day I considered that I wasn't so happy with my life. Something was wrong, something was missing. As St. Augustine says, "You have made us for yourself, O Lord, and our hearts are restless until they rest in You." For all its splendor, the world cannot satisfy the deepest longings of the heart for perfect life, truth, and love. Yet, the world teaches hedonism through the media—the lie that we can find happiness in pleasures, possessions and self-indulgence.

The Spiritual Heart Chart

This early reflection about my life and my lack of happiness, led me to later develop what I call the spiritual heart chart. In my convert classes I teach this understanding of the depths of our heart and its need for God. This Spiritual Heart Chart is a graphic representation of the four loves in life, listed in their proper priority: God first, my neighbor or human love-including self—is second, third is my physical comfort and consolations, and my material comforts are last. It is basically a group of four circles, with the one in the center representing the most intimate and deepest love of the heart. I explain that this shows the spiritual layers of our heart. The way it should be is for God to be in the center circle, the next outer ring is for our family and friends, the next level is for sensual pleasures, and the outermost circle represents our possessions. Ideally, God is to be in the center of our hearts and our lives, as the highest priority, but when sin enters our lives the priority changes.

In a life of serious sin, in the center of our heart can be sensual pleasures, material possessions, or even the love of self or other humans, and God is pushed to the outer circle inverting the natural priority in our lives. All that which is truly good in our lives comes from God, and is given to help us, not to replace the true God of heaven, with the earthly idols of flesh and steel. Scripture says, "*I have no good apart from thee*" (Ps.16). Scripture teaches us the priority of the four loves:

God is first,

"But seek first his kingdom and his righteousness, and all these things shall be yours as well." (Matt. 6:19-21,31-33) "You have been told, O man, what is good, and what the Lord requires of you; only to do the right and to love goodness, and to walk humbly with your God." (Mic.6:8)

Our neighbor is second,
"You shall love your neighbor as yourself." (Mt.22:37-39), but still subordinate to our love of God, "He who loves father or mother more than me is not worthy of me..." (Mt.10:37), "For in the resurrection they neither marry...but are like angels in heaven." (Mt.22:30, also: 1Cor.7:29)

The third priority is our bodily desires, which cannot satisfy and do not belong in the center of our heart or lives. Scripture teaches the limitations of sensual pleasures, "...the eye is not satisfied with seeing, nor the ear filled with hearing." (Ec.1:8).

And, the fourth and least important love is our material things, "...a man's life does not consist in the abundance of his possessions." (Lk.12:15) "For what does it profit a man, if he gain the whole world, and suffer the loss of his own soul?" (Mt.16:26)

Since there is no way for the lesser loves to compete with God, and those who invert the priorities of their heart actually know this in a basic way, they try to make up the difference through excess. To substitute the love of self, of friends, of bodily pleasures, and of possessions for the love of God, means these things will fall short because they are lacking in themselves. However, the sinner is also a fool, and so he seeks to amplify and multiply these finite things by increasing them, as if this would some how make them compete with the infinite love of God! Sensing their shortcomings against the natural longing for the infinite within our hearts, sin calls us to try to sin more as if it would make things better. And so, the drunkard drinks more, the drug addict takes more drugs, the fornicator fornicates more, and the materialist seeks to own more, as if this multiplication of it will cause it to be more than it is. It cannot be more than God, because it is less than God. Yet, the world is filled with people who choose to invert the natural priorities of love, and place everything else above God. And, when they find that these things do not give happiness, they turn to cynicism, despair, and are tempted into suicide, and depression and other forms of escape. They are willing to try any path, but prayer, to serve any idol instead of the one true God. All these false paths seem to cry out to man's soul, "I cannot satisfy you, you are meant for more than me, seek the God who created us all, and don't try to make the created things your god." Instead of picking up the bottle of booze or whatever your sinful weakness is, pick up the rosary of grace!

The Montfortian Promise

Although as an adolescent, my understanding of these truths was not so developed, I still knew the basic message that happiness comes through closeness to God. The closer we are to God the happier we are, the farther from him we get the sadder we are. After much thinking I realized that I was happy as a child because I was closer to God. As an adolescent I was drifting farther away by the day. I realized that the saints were close to God because they prayed so much.

Our parents can take us only so far in the faith, eventually we must decide for ourselves whether to persevere on the right road. I decided it was time for me to pray. I knew how to pray only one prayer—the Rosary. I went and took my mother's Rosary off her dresser and began to pray it. I prayed it every day for a few weeks. I began to feel closer to God and I even dared to ask for something. To my surprise my prayer was answered and I realized that God was truly there. Coincidence could not explain the answer to my prayer because it happened at precisely the time and in precisely the way I had requested it. At this point, I realized that God was not just there, but ready, willing and able to help me and participate in my life as a great friend (Jn.15:15), as an invisible but loving Father.

Daily prayer is the way God calls everyone to live out a relationship with Him. When my dad saw my interest in the Rosary, he gave me a book by St. Louis de Montfort, *The Secret of the Rosary.* One may ask, "Is the pen still mightier than the sword?" If I reflect upon the power of books to change lives and influence the world, it certainly seems so. Many conversions to the Lord have come through books, and my own is no exception. When I was fourteen, I was very concerned about finding a sure and certain way to get to Heaven. I think God saw what I was looking for and provided it for me in this book. In it was a line that helped motivate me to persevere in the Rosary, and changed my life. I felt this was it. I had a Saint promising me if I did something, it would be the surest way to heaven. I have since dubbed it the Montfortian Promise. I know that except by a special revelation of God, we cannot be certain we will be saved because we cannot be sure of the grace of final perseverance. Regardless of how much we pray, and how much grace we have, concupiscence is always with us,

"...the imagination and thought of man's heart are prone to evil from his youth." (Gen.8:21) "Watch and pray that you may not enter into temptation; the spirit indeed is willing, but the flesh is weak." (Mt.26:41) Even the great St. Paul says: "But I chastise my body, and bring it into subjection: lest perhaps, after I have preached to others, I myself should become lost." (1Cor.9:27) Even the great King David who was so close to God in his youth, fell into adultery and murder (2Sa.12:9), yet the Lord forgave him. Proclaiming the mercy of God for generations, the first line of the New Testament calls, "*Jesus Christ, the Son of David.*" (Mt.1:1). However, I know that reading these lines of St. Louis inspired me like no other:

"If you say the Rosary faithfully until death, I do assure you that, in spite of the gravity of your sins "*you shall receive a never fading crown of glory.*" (1Pt.5:4) Even if you are on the brink of damnation, even if you have one foot in hell, even if you have sold your soul to the devil as sorcerers do who practice black magic, and even if you are a heretic as obstinate as a devil, sooner or later you will be converted and will amend your life and save your soul, if—and mark well what I say—if you say the Holy Rosary devoutly every day until death for the purpose of knowing the truth and obtaining contrition and pardon for your sins." (*The Secret of the Rosary*, by St. Louis Mary De Montfort, Montfort Publications, Bay Shore, N.Y. 11706, pg.12)

This was my first encounter with spiritual reading, something we should all be doing on a regular basis. This wonderful book inspired me so much, I was determined to never abandon the Rosary. Since the age of fourteen, I have prayed almost without fail the fifteen decades of the Rosary each day. Unfortunately however, there were a few times I strayed from prayer. The few times I have abandoned the Rosary through worldly faulty reasoning, I have at the very least lost a sense of spiritual peace in my soul, and at worst lapsed into sins.

Having been raised in the sixties and seventies, I was greatly influenced by television. I learned logic from First Officer Spock, manliness from James Bond, and sarcasm from Bugs Bunny! Despite the influence of the world the flesh and the devil on our souls, the power and influence of God in the world is still greater, as scripture says: "*...for he who is in you is greater than he who is in the world.*" (1Jn.4:4) "*In the world you have tribulation; but be of good cheer, I have overcome the world.*" (Jn.16:33). However, it is up to us to respond to His grace to change. Prayer helps us push out of our heart the false gods of flesh and steel. "*Put to death* *therefore what is earthly in you: immorality, impurity, passion, evil desire, and covetousness, which is idolatry."* (Col.3:5). In time, after praying the Rosary as a teenager, the lure of beautiful women, fast cars, and automatic weapons was decreased, and the love of the Rosary, the Scriptures, and the Holy Eucharist was increased!

With Mary We Never Pray Alone

When we need help the most, we don't just go directly to God alone, we ask others to pray for us and with us. When we pray the Rosary, we have Mary, the Holy Mother of God, pray to God for us and with us. God wishes us to honor Mary because of her special role in God's plan of salvation. She contributed to the redemption of Man just as Eve contributed to the fall of man. Mary is our spiritual Mother and we grow in grace when we honor her in a spiritual way. *"Whoever glorifies his mother is like one who lays up treasure."* (Sir.3:4,5) Mary and Jesus are not in competition for our soul or its affection, they are on the same team, working together.

Interestingly enough, I actually did try to pray to God six months before I started the Rosary in August of 1977. I started to try to pray several Our Fathers each day, but for some reason I didn't persevere. I believe it was because I needed the extra prayers of Our Lady on top of mine, to get the graces necessary to win my heart back from the world. When I tried praying alone I didn't persevere. When I prayed with Our Lady her prayers helped give me the grace I needed to persevere. This is why I get so bewildered and frustrated by those who keep saying they want to go directly to God alone, and don't want the prayers and help of their spiritual mother who was given to them by God. If it weren't for Mary's extra help and prayers that year, I'm not sure if I ever would have come to any significant knowledge or relationship with Christ.

Mary is Our Spiritual Helpmate

It was truly Mary who led me to Jesus; it was she who helped "save" me by praying those extra graces I needed at that time into my life. And, that is her role. Eve failed as a "helpmate" (Gen.2:18) to Adam. Mary is the perfect "helpmate" (Lk.1:38) to Christ, and this is especially true in his mystical body - the Church. God has chosen her to be the helpmate of the mystical body of Christ. Scripture says:

*It is not good that the man is alone; I will make him a helpmate. (*Gen. 2:18)

Behold the handmaid of the Lord. (Luke 1:38)

The job of praying for us to get closer to Her Son and be saved is assigned by God to Mary. God prepared her for this special role through the Immaculate Conception, which enabled her to be the true victorious "replacement" of Eve. Unlike Eve who was defeated, Our Lady is victorious over the devil. Our Lord delights in humiliating him continuously through the centuries, through the sinless virgin working as our primary prayer intercessor for the Church—for everyone fighting for salvation here on earth. After all, he *chose* to begin his public ministry and work his first miracle through her intercession (Jn.2:1-12).

Christ is our only mediator (1Tim.2:5-6) with the Father, but Mary can intercede (pray for us) with her Son Jesus. Just as we can ask others members of the church on earth to pray for us (1Tim.2:1, 2Tim.1:3, Phil4, 22), so, too, we can ask members of the church in heaven to pray for us (Rev.5:8, 6:9-11, 7:10-12, 8:2-6, Mat.22:31, 32). As a builder is honored when someone admires his work, God is honored when we honor Mary. As a Father is pleased when his daughter is honored, God loves us to honor Mary. All the honor we give to Mary is reflected back to God since we honor her for what He has done for her, with her, and through her. When we honor her we honor Him.

Mary's role as the Mother of Christ did not end on earth, her faithful service on earth prepared her for her new role in heaven (Rev.12:1) as the Mother of the Mystical Body of Christ. And, that is why *"the dragon was angry with the woman, and went off to make war on the rest of her offspring, on those who keep the commandments of God and bear testimony to Jesus."* (Rev.12:17). And, that is why the Rosary works so well, because it is the plan of God for his adopted sons (Gal.4:5, Jn.1:12) to have the prayers of their adopted spiritual mother. And, where does the power come from other than God himself! God prepared Mary for this role at the Immaculate Conception and the Rosary is the prayer given by God that helps us tap into the power of the Immaculate Conception, like no other.

Catholics worship only God, but they honor Mary as their spiritual Mother (Rev.12:1-17, Jn.19:26,27). We are commanded by God to *"Honor your Father and Mother"* (Ex.20:12), thus the honor we give to Mary our Spiritual Mother in no way subtracts from the worship we give to God any more than honoring our earthly mother does. In fact, it conforms to God's holy will, and we who are sons of God honor her whom the Son of God honored. The devil seeks to blind Christians from the special connection between God and Mary, and he quotes scripture in this temptation, just as he did when he misinterpreted it when he tempted Christ (Mt.4:5,6). As he misquoted scripture to try to trick Christ, he misquotes scripture to try to trick his followers.. As the misinterpretation of the Old Testament made Christ a *"stumbling block"*(1Cor.1:23) to the Jews, the misinterpretation of the New Testament has made Mary a "stumbling block" to some Christians. Mary is a *"stone rejected by the builders"* (Mt.21:42), the builders of the protestant reformation. And we know it's not the Holy Spirit that's in charge of misinterpreting scripture, since it was the Holy Spirit that inspired the scriptures. It is of great interest to the devil to keep Christians from praying the Rosary because this prayer was especially prepared by God to be the surest, fastest, safest, and easiest way to bring souls into his Kingdom. This concept is taught in *True Devotion to Mary* by St. Louis De Montfort. Many have discovered Jesus as their Savior, but they need to discover Mary as their Mother. If we are truly in the family of God, then we have our Heavenly Father as our provider, Jesus as our Savior, the Holy Spirit as our indwelling sanctifier, and Mary as our praying spiritual mother (Rev.12:17). The miracle of the Rosary lies in its power to transform the lives of men from being servants of the world, into saints of God.

Mary is Our Mother in the Family of God

There's something wrong with a family if it doesn't have both a father and a mother. God's family has its Perfect Heavenly Father and its Immaculate Heavenly Mother. Why is she our Mother? Because, God chose to make her *His* mother and *Our* mother. The last gift to us from Christ was His mother. He gave her to us from the cross with his dying breath. At the foot of the cross Jesus told Mary she would now have spiritual children to in addition to Jesus, when he said, *"Woman, behold your son!"* (Jn.19:26) These words taught Mary that she would now have a new relationship with her son's disciples. What he said to St. John he said to us all, *"Behold, your mother!"* (Jn.19:27) St. John later wrote *"the dragon was angry with the woman, and went off to make war on the rest of her offspring, on those who keep the commandments of God and bear testimony to Jesus.*" (Rev.12:17) God's family is not unnatural, it is not without a mother. God is our heavenly Father and Mary is our spiritual Mother. Scripture says, "*But to all who received him, who believed in his name, he gave power to become children of God*" (Jn.1:12) When Jesus dwells within us, we are sons of the Father like him, and we also become a "*son of Mary*" (Mk.6:3) like him. When Jesus dwells within us we are, like him, the sons and daughters in the Eternal Family of God.

In marriage life begins in the Father and is nurtured in the mother. So too, in the spiritual life it begins with God the Father, but is nurtured by the prayers of our spiritual Mother. The instrument of this supernatural nurturing is the Rosary. The Church is the family of God (Eph.3:15) and Mary is the mother of the Church. Mary gave birth to Christ, and the Church is the mystical body of Christ (1Cor.12:27), and so Mary is the Mystical mother of the Church (Rev.12:2,17). Let your participation in God's family be complete: love and honor your heavenly Father and Mother in the way God has chosen, through the daily rosary.

The Rosary is the family prayer of the family of God. What is a family without a mother? The Church is "*the Body of Christ*" (Eph.1:23, 1Cor.12:27), and "*the Family of God*" (Eph.3:15). Christ must honor his mother perfectly to perfectly keep the commandment, "*Honor your father and mother*" and this is exactly what the Body of Christ, the Church, does when it honors Mary. When the Church honors Mary, it is Christ honoring His mother, it is the family of God honoring its Mother, the Mother of God—the Mother of the Mystical body of Christ.

The Rosary combines the meditation on the life of Jesus and Mary with the worship of the Father (Mt.6:6), the Honor of Mary, and the prayers of Mary in heaven united with our prayers on earth. This Honor of Mary is first commanded by the Father through the Archangel Gabriel (Lk.1:29) and given by the Holy Spirit in scripture (Lk.1:42) and tradition. Mary is the Mother of Jesus and Our Spiritual Mother and her prayers are the most powerful prayers of the highest saint in heaven who is not just any saint, but our adopted spiritual mother! Jesus combines the supernatural power of prayer with the natural power of the love of a mother, to give us the most powerful prayers in heaven every time we pray the Rosary.

It is no wonder the devil works so hard to keep us away from this prayer, because so many graces are available through it that do not come through any other prayer. When we pray the Rosary we retrieve the power of the Immaculate Conception, the victory of Christ over the devil given to

Mary when God created her. This was Satan's great defeat, God prepared a replacement for Eve, another sinless virgin created by God. She was to be the one perfect disciple of Christ, the first to believe in Him, the first to touch Him, and the one chosen by God to pray for us on earth, and in heaven. Through the Rosary we have the most powerful saint in heaven, Mary, the one conceived without sin who never sinned, praying for us and with us, whenever we ask.

God had the rare privilege of being able to choose and create his own mother. He chose the soul he knew would be most faithful to him, and he created her without sin. No other person in history was created without sin, but no other person in history was chosen by God to conceive by the Holy Spirit and give birth to the Son of God. The Immaculate Conception is unique, but that is because the role of Mary is unique. As a builder is honored when someone admires his work, God honored when we honor Mary. God loves us to honor Mary as a Father is pleased when his daughter is honored. All the honor we give to Mary is reflected back to God since we honor her for what He has done for her, with her, and through her. When we honor her we honor Him.

I often preach on the Rosary and make it an essential part of my priestly ministry. One of my parishioners who noticed this jokingly called me, "Captain Rosary!" So great have been the graces and favors given to me by Our Lady through the Rosary that I have dedicated my life to spreading the Rosary devotion. In any way I can, by prayer, word, and example, I seek to encourage others to discover the hidden treasure of the Rosary in their lives as I have discovered it in mine. It is a pearl of great price (Mt.13:46) that can give spiritual beauty and life to anyone who will receive it. It is a spiritual pearl that will make its owners rich in grace, knowledge, and love of God. It is a seed that can yield a hundredfold (Mt.13:8) of fruits in the Holy Spirit. It is a powerful means to obtain a deep and fulfilling relationship with Jesus Christ. It helps one grow in all areas of the spiritual life, and is the perfect companion to the Holy Scripture and the Holy Eucharist. If I could, I would place a Rosary in the hand of every man and woman on the face of the earth. Pope St. Pius IX said,"Give me an army praying the Rosary, and I will conquer the world."

Chapter 2

When and Where
to Pray the Rosary

"But standing by the cross of Jesus were his mother... When Jesus saw his mother, and the disciple whom he loved standing near, he said to his mother, 'Woman, behold, your son!' Then he said to the disciple, 'Behold, your mother!'" (John 19:25-27)

Praying With Mary At the Foot of the Cross

Prayer is often very effective when the cross is near us or upon us. The cross is the condition of Christ's discipleship. It includes all the suffering and hardship involved in resisting temptation, keeping the commandments, and doing the physical and spiritual works of mercy. *"If anyone wishes to come after me, let him deny himself, and take up his cross daily, and follow me."* (Lk.9:23, 1Cor.1:18) The beauty of the Rosary is that we can pray it in the most inconvenient situations, when we are alone and suffering or when with others who are suffering. Once we know how to pray it, the Rosary is so simple, we don't even have to have the beads with us, we can simply count on our fingers or in our minds.

When we are struggling and suffering Jesus tells us we don't need to pray alone, he says, *"Behold, your mother!"* (Jn.19:27) When children are hurt and cry, they run to their mothers' arms. Though we may be old men, we are always children of God, and he has given us his mother to be our mother. God has appointed her to be our spiritual helper, to comfort us and pray with us in time of need. The devil knows our strengths and weaknesses and uses them against us. God knows our strengths and weaknesses and uses them to help save us. Since we are in this intense spiritual battle for our eternal souls, why go it alone? Why not enlist the help of a powerful ally, our spiritual mother, the one handpicked by God for the job. It is perhaps to foster greater humiliation to Satan that God gives so much power in heaven to a simple maiden who served God on earth as a wife and mother. The full reason for God's choice will not be revealed to us in this life, but Jesus says, *"you will know them by their fruits"* (Mt.7:16). The fruits of devotion to Mary are greater love for God and neighbor.

Sanctifying Idle Time

The Rosary enables us to sanctify idle time. It is such a simple prayer we can pray it at almost any time and under any circumstances. Although praying in church has certain advantages, such as the presence of the Blessed Sacrament, we don't have to be in church to pray. Our bodies are the temples of the Holy Spirit, so wherever we are, we can pray. Jesus said,

"...the hour is coming when neither on this mountain nor in Jerusalem will you worship the Father... But the hour is coming, and now is, when the true worshipers will worship the Father in spirit and truth, for such the Father seeks to worship him. God is spirit, and those who worship him must worship in spirit and truth." (Jn.4:21-24)

When we pray the Rosary we worship in the Holy Spirit with the Truth of God's Holy Word and the truths of the Holy Gospel.

When I went through basic training at Lackland A.F.B. in Texas, we spent many hours marching in the heat of July. In basic training it felt like time moved so slowly: every second was like a minute, every minute was like an hour, every hour was like a day. Time may fly when you're having fun, but it almost stops when you're in misery! I can remember the sweat pouring down my back so fast it was like a small river. To help my sanity and my soul, I secretly counted on my fingers each decade of the Rosary. By the end of the day of marching and other activities, I had done fifteen decades or more, despite the yelling of my Training Instructor! The Rosary gave me a sense of inner peace, and helped me endure those six weeks of Basic Training.

When we go for a health walk during the evening or the day, we can pray the Rosary. I call it *Rosary Aerobics*, exercise for the body and the soul. Even if we are just going for a stroll we can be a *holy stroller!* We can pray sitting or in a nice rocking chair on the porch we can be a *holy rocker!* We can also sanctify our commute to work. Many times on a long drive on the interstate I get the Rosary done very easily. It takes only a little grace and inspiration to turn off that radio for a while, and give some time to God in prayer. Many people pray a decade or more each day on the way to work or school, I call them *Holy Rollers!* I don't recommend praying in busy city traffic where high concentration is necessary for safe driving, but rather on a low traffic highway where we can pray and drive safely. My dream is for the world to be filled with *holy strollers, holy rockers, and holy rollers!*

So, we now have an answer to the question,"Where do we pray?" We may pray at home in our room (Mt.6:1-6, Mk.1:35), at Church with our family (Mt.21:13), while riding in a car or anywhere. Through prayer we can sanctify idle moments and give that extra free time to God. On where to pray Jesus said, alone in a private place is a very good place to pray. Solitude in prayer fosters concentration, and spiritual intimacy with God:

"But when you pray, go into your room and shut the door and pray to your Father who is in secret; and your Father who sees in secret will reward you." (Mt.6:6) "And in the morning, a great while before day, he rose and went out to a lonely place, and there he prayed."(Mk.1:35)

He also taught the goodness of praying with others, especially in the Church, the house of prayer:

"And he taught, and said to them, "Is it not written, 'My house shall be called a house of prayer for all the nations?'..." (Mk.11:17) "Again I say to you, if two of you agree on earth about anything they ask, it will be done for them by my Father in heaven. For where two or three are gathered in my name, there am I in the midst of them." (Mt.18:20)

One of the best places to pray the Rosary is in Church, especially if the Blessed Sacrament is Exposed. When we pray the Rosary with others, graces are multiplied, and we share in the grace from each Rosary. The Church offers us an indulgence for the recitation of the Marian Rosary:

"A *plenary indulgence* is granted when the rosary is recited in a church or oratory or when it is recited in a family, a religious community, or a pious association. A *partial indulgence* is granted for its recitation in all other circumstances." (Pg. 79. *The Handbook of Indulgences, Norms and Grants,* Authorized English Edition, copyright 1991, Catholic Book Publishing Co., N.Y.)

The Rosary Challenge — A Decade a Day

"And I tell you, Ask, and it will be given you; seek, and you will find; knock, and it will be opened to you." (Luke 11:9)

You should begin to pray the Rosary on a daily basis by praying just a decade each day, until you feel you want to pray more. You should try one decade a day for a week or two until you feel comfortable enough to try more. Let the Rosary grow on you, get used to it gradually. Some who are comfortable doing five decades right away should do so. I do not wish to restrict anyone from praying more, only to make it easier for people starting so they don't get discouraged. Usually people pray 5 decades a day once they are used to it, since that would complete one set of the four types of Mysteries. You may later want to pray 5 decades a day as you get used to the prayer. All who pray the Rosary should experience a profound outpouring of grace. Even a decade a day starts the graces flowing. I have a saying, "A decade a day keeps the devil away!"

If you are a person reading this now who has never tried the Rosary for a month or so, I challenge you to pray the Rosary. Even if you do only one decade a day for a month you should try it. See if you do not detect the peace, grace, and love of God increase noticeably in your life within one month. Most people notice an increase in inner peace. What would it hurt to spend a few minutes in this great biblical prayer, recommended by Saints and heaven itself for just a month? Give our Lord and Our Lady a chance to touch you with special graces. Try the Rosary for one month, I guarantee you will never regret it. When you enter into eternity you will bless the day and hour when you took my advice — or rather should I say the advice I took from the Saints and the Mother of God. Indeed, it is actually the message given by God himself to all of them — pray the Rosary every day until death so that you may most safely, and surely, hear these words, "Come, O blessed of my Father, inherit the kingdom prepared for you from the foundation of the world." (Mt. 25:34) You will count the time spent on earth praying the Rosary as among the most valuable things done. For the Rosary powerfully unlocks the graces of worthy reception of the sacraments, gives us strength to keep the commandments, and persevere in the fourteen works of mercy.

The Rosary Decision

Of all the decisions I have made in my life none was more important than my decision to pray the rosary every day. No decision I have made in my life has affected me more profoundly, more positively, more deeply, and more enduringly, than to pray the Rosary every day. Though I am still indeed a sinner with many failures and weaknesses, who prays the Rosary, I know that without the Rosary, I would now be much more selfish, much more sinful, and much further from God and all that is good. I shudder to think how my life would be if I had not chosen to pray the Rosary. Indeed, I might not even be alive, but instead be in the *"everlasting fire prepared for the devil and his angels."* (Mt.25:41) Were it not for the love God showed me by giving me the grace to choose the Rosary, my life would have been completely different, and probably completely ruined. Though I have had misfortuncs and disasters to deal with, they would have been much worse without the Rosary. Though I have fallen into many sins, they would have been much worse without the Rosary.

I can offer no one any greater advice than to *"pray the Rosary every day"* (the words of Our Lady of Fatima). Nor does the greatest saint in heaven, the Mother of God, offer any greater advice. This is the simple yet great message that the Son of God sent St. Mary his Mother, back to earth at Fatima, Lourdes, and other places to tell us all *"pray the Rosary every day."*

The Rosary is a great spiritual key that unlocks a treasure chest of graces which we could not have without Our Lady's prayers joined to ours. The Rosary is a fearsome spiritual weapon against sin that Satan tries to blind the world from knowledge of either its existence or its value. Trying to serve God without the Rosary is like flying in a propellor plane toward heaven and trying to serve God with the Rosary is like flying in a supersonic jet toward heaven. This is why St. Louis De Montfort describes true devotion to Our Lady, (of which the daily Rosary is the heart of this devotion), as the quickest, safest, and best way to spiritual union with Our Lord. The Rosary is the *"pearl of great value"* (Mt.13:46) that has been hidden in the Gospel. Praying it makes the words and events of the Gospel come to life in our soul. Let us set a goal to pray the Rosary daily, at least one decade each day, and to daily *"Greet Mary who has worked hard among you."* (Rom. 16:6)

The Beauty of the Beads

The Rosary itself is a beautiful concrete symbol of prayer. Seeing a rosary on a night stand next to a bed is a symbol that the soul is dedicated to God. The Rosary itself is a reminder that we have prayed, and that we should pray. Although prayer is not something concrete, but a spiritual action of the soul, the rosary is possibly the closest thing we have in sacramentals to prayer in the form of matter. Each bead is a reminder of prayer, and the crucifix at the end of the beads is a reminder of who we pray to. Pope John Paul II says:

"As a true apostle of the Rosary, Blessed Bartolo Longo had a special charism. His path to holiness rested on an inspiration heard in the depths of his heart: "Whoever spreads the Rosary is saved!"... The traditional aid used for the recitation of the Rosary is the set of beads. At the most superficial level, the beads often become a simple counting mechanism to mark the succession of Hail Marys. Yet they can also take on a symbolism which can give added depth to contemplation. Here the first thing to note is the way the beads converge upon the Crucifix, which both opens and closes the unfolding sequence of prayer. The life and prayer of believers is centered upon Christ. Everything begins from him, everything leads towards him, everything, through him, in the Holy Spirit, attains to the Father. As a counting mechanism, marking the progress of the prayer, the beads evoke the unending path of contemplation and of Christian perfection. Blessed Bartolo Longo saw them also as a "chain" which links us to God. A chain, yes, but a sweet chain; for sweet indeed is the bond to God who is also our Father." (Apostolic Letter Rosarium Virginis Mariae, Copyright Libreria Editrice Vaticana)

The Rosary is a Holistic Prayer

The Rosary engages our heart, mind, body, and soul all at once, so there is a holistic healing therapy which comes through the Rosary. Oftentimes meditation helps us with our nervousness. The simple calm rhythmic repeating of the Our Father and the Hail Mary, coupled with the gliding of the beads through our fingers, helps us emotionally, mentally, and spiritually. The Rosary beads are actually a physical and emotional help to meditation. Part of prayer and meditation is being calm and letting the peace of Christ fill our hearts and minds. The Rosary beads displace nervous energy and actually help us calm down. The simple physical feeling of the beads flowing through our hands as we pray, helps us reduce our anxiety level.

If we are anxious our anxiety should lead us to pray over what is causing the anxiety. The rosary will help us gain a sense of peace and a sense of purpose in our lives. We all have a natural anxiety over the things we worry about. Through prayer we can present them to God and relieve some of that anxiety. I find I am often like Martha in the Bible, to whom our Lord said, "Martha, Martha, you are anxious and troubled about many things; one thing is needful..." (Lk.10:41,42, see also Mt.6:25-34) And, that one thing needed is salvation. The rosary will help us with both our anxiety and our salvation.

Whether we are sitting or walking the beads are actually an aid to prayer and meditation. After all, this prayer comes from the same God who made our body and our soul, and it is designed to connect and work with both at once.

The rosary beads are used to help count the prayers as we pray the rosary. The beads enable our mind to be more free to concentrate on the prayers and meditations. The use of the beads is recommended by Mary herself, through her example. When she appeared at Lourdes and Fatima, the visionaries recall the beads passing through her fingers as they prayed their rosaries. Some priests who have been imprisoned in communist countries or during wartime prayed using their ten fingers to count the prayers. In a sense our hands are natural emergency rosary beads!

My aunt sent me a beautiful little poem she found on the Rosary. It is called:

My Rosary Beads

A little pair of Rosary beads
as plain as plain can be.
But only God in Heaven knows
how dear they are to me.
I have them always with me
At every step I take.
At evening when I slumber,

At morning when I wake.
In bright and cloudy weather,
In sunshine or n rain.
In happiness or in sorrow,
In pleasure or in pain.
It helps me in my struggle,
It reproves me when in sin.
Its look of gentle patience
Rebukes the strife within.
In days of pain and anguish,
The greatest help I knew,
Was to hold my Rosary Beads,
Until I calmer grew.
So when the time approaches,
When I will have to die.
I hope my little Rosary Beads
Will close beside me lie.
That the Holy Name of Jesus,
May be the last I say,
And kissing my Rosary Beads,
My Soul will pass away.
(Author Unknown)

Chapter 3

Don't let Distractions get you down

"So, leaving them again, he went away and prayed for the third time the same words." (Mt.26:44)

Devotion Versus Distraction

Prayer is often difficult, even a battle—to start and to persevere. Prayer is also called lifting our hearts and minds to God. As our hearts rise to God's, and our minds rise to his, there are many blocks and much turbulence along the way. This struggle is a daily reminder of how far we have fallen from original grace. Prayer is all about restoring that grace, and pushing the flesh and the world from our hearts and minds is a lifelong struggle. Prayer is a spiritual labor of the love of God and, it is not always easy to pray.

Devotion is putting our hearts into our prayers. Scripture reminds us of its importance, *"This people honors me with their lips, but their heart is far from me."* (Mt.15:18) When we are desperate for help it is often easier to do, however we must realize we are always desperate for more grace. It is better to say one Hail Mary properly with attention and devotion, than a hundred rushed without devotion and while distracted. It is better to pray five decades of the Rosary slowly with attention and devotion, than to pray 15 decades quickly and when distracted . It is not quantity, it is quality in prayer that Our Lord seeks. However, we must not go to the other extreme where we become so scrupulous that we get discouraged and hardly pray at all or spend only a short time in prayer. There needs to be a balance between the two.

I have been praying the Rosary for 29 years and yet, I have never said a perfect rosary and I probably never will. I have always had distractions. Nevertheless, the rosary gets prayed and God hears it and answers with graces and favors. The Lord knows we are not perfect, but he expects us to continue to strive for spiritual perfection: *"You, therefore, must be perfect, as your heavenly Father is perfect."* (Mt.5:48)

The Battle to Persevere in Prayer

We were drafted into God's army at Baptism, and we are all part of Heaven's war engaging in spiritual combat on earth. Our primary mission is to persevere in prayer, despite the enemys' constant war of distractions, discouragement, dryness in prayer, and prayers which *seem* to be unanswered.

The Catechism of the Catholic Church says:

"...prayer is a battle. Against whom? Against ourselves and against the wiles of the tempter who does all he can to turn man away from prayer, away from union with God.... The habitual difficulty in prayer is *distraction*.... To set about hunting down distractions would be to fall into their trap, when all that is necessary is to turn back to our heart, for a distraction reveals to us what we are attached to, and this humble awareness before the Lord should awaken our preferential love for him and lead us resolutely to offer him our hearts to be purified. Therein lies the battle, the choice of which master to serve... When we begin to pray, a thousand labors or cares thought to be urgent vie for priority; once again, it is the moment of truth for the heart; what is its real love?" (CCC 2725, 2729, 2732)

Prayer is a sacrifice of our time and will. Repetition is hard, but it helps us sacrifice our will and our time to be humble and submissive to God's word. It is a challenge to repeat, over and over, what we have not yet fully achieved, but strive for daily. And, we achieve more and more with each repetition. Namely, we are loving God with our whole heart, soul, mind, and strength.

The devil, the spiritual enemy of our soul and of prayer, seeks to make us abandon prayer and meditation, by plying us with distractions. St. Teresa of Avila says that the soul which perseveres in mental prayer is lost to the devil, and so he seeks to make us despair in prayer and give up on account of dryness and distractions. We must remember the Lord will reward his faithful lovers who prove their love by persevering in a lifelong struggle to pray in the midst of the battlefield of distraction and aridity.

When we persevere in prayer and meditation, even during the worst distractions, it is not a waste of time but a proof of love. Our love of God was lost through sin, but it is to be regained through battle, a great spiritual battle against our own weakened nature. A certain degree of involuntary distractions is inevitable, however, we must continue to work during prayer to minimize them. We must not go to the other extreme of making no effort to deal with distractions. It is important to pay attention to the words we pray. Do not stop praying because of distractions, but do not stop returning to the Lord once you discover your mind drifting in prayer. Enter into the spiritual battle as a soldier, or your soul will be slaughtered as a bystander. Let prayer transform your anxiety into devotion. Pray to God about what worries you and you will worry less:

"Have no anxiety about anything, but in everything by prayer and supplication with thanksgiving let your requests be made known to God. And the peace of God, which passes all understanding, will keep your hearts and your minds in Christ Jesus." (Phil.4:6, 7)

If you feel you were distracted during a *Hail Mary* or an *Our Father* don't go backwards and redo it, simply continue praying and work on doing better on the next one. This is a scrupulous trap the devil sets for beginners, if we follow it to its full illogical conclusion we might never finish praying. We will always have some prayers we do with more attention than others. We should set a reasonable pace.

Sometimes people pray the rosary so fast when leading the rosary in a group, they sound like an auctioneer! They can sound like they are in a hurry to get it over with. We do not want to pray the prayer so fast it is difficult to concentrate on their meaning, especially when we pray the rosary out loud in a group. If we are praying by ourselves silently we may find ourselves drawn into the layers of spiritual meanings of each word and praying them more slowly and contemplatively. When praying in a group we should not set a pace that is unreasonably fast or slow, and when praying silently alone, we should maintain a pace that is comfortable for our minds to properly absorb the words and their meanings. We can set our own pace for ourselves when we pray alone. Sometimes we may want to pray more slowly, sometimes more quickly, it depends on the individual. We should pray at our own pace, as long as we are not racing or praying so fast we can't even think about the words we are saying.

Every Hail Mary has great value:

"Blessed Alan says that a nun who had always had great devotion to the Holy Rosary appeared after her death to one of her sisters in religion and said to her: 'If I were allowed to go back into my body, to have the chance of saying just one single Hail Mary—even if I said it quickly and without great fervor—I would gladly go through the sufferings that I had during my last illness all over again, in order to gain the merit of this prayer.'...This is all the more compelling because she had been bedridden and had suffered agonizing pains for several years before she died." (*The Secret of the Rosary*, by St. Louis Mary De Montfort, Montfort Publications, Bay Shore, N.Y. 11706, pg.49, 50)

The Power of Repetition

Jesus taught us that we need to have attention to the words we speak to God in prayer, and not simply say many words "*And in praying do not heap up empty phrases as the Gentiles do; for they think that they will be heard for their many words.*" (Mt.6:7) However, the Bible teaches that repetitious prayer is good. In his most critical hour of need, Jesus himself prayed repetitious prayer when he repeated his same phrase to the Father three times. "*...he fell on his face and prayed, 'My Father, if it be possible, let this cup pass from me; nevertheless, not as I will but as thou wilt.'... So, leaving them again, he went away and prayed for the third time the same words.*" (Mt.26:44) It is not logically possible to interpret (Mt.6:7) as condemning repetitious prayer since Jesus used this method and there are many prayers in scripture that are litanies. Daniel 3:52-90, Psalm 117 and Psalm 136 repeat the same phrases many times. Psalm 136 repeats 26 times in its total 26 verses, "*His steadfast love endures for ever,*" and Psalm150 repeats "*Praise him*" six times in the six verses that make up the whole Psalm. We see in scripture the beauty of repetitious prayer in the stories in Luke 18:9-14 and Mark 10:46-52. Repetitious prayer is so important and valuable, even the angels who are worthy to surround his throne are commanded by God to pray in repetitious prayer,

"I saw the Lord sitting upon a throne, high and lifted up; and his train filled the temple. Above him stood the seraphim; each had six wings... And one called to another and said: 'Holy, holy, holy is the Lord of hosts; the whole earth is full of his glory.' And the foundations of the thresholds shook at the voice of him who called, and the house was filled with smoke." (Is.6:1-4)

"...day and night they never cease to sing, 'Holy, holy, holy, is the Lord God Almighty, who was and is and is to come!'" (Rev.4:8)

When we pray the Rosary we pray like the angels in heaven. After all, the "Hail Mary" is called the "Angelic Salutation". Repetitious prayer is also called a *litany*, and in the Rosary each decade consists of a litany of Hail Marys done with a meditation on a different holy mystery from the Gospel. In the beautiful litanous prayer of the Rosary, we repeat the words of Our Lord (Mt.6:9-13), the words of the Archangel (Lk.1:28), and the words of the Holy Spirit spoken through St. Elizabeth (Lk.1:42) and through the Sacred Tradition of the Church.

The late great Archbishop Fulton J. Sheen, Servant of God, once wrote about the repetition in the Rosary. In his book *The World's First Love* (copyright 1952, Fulton J.Sheen, Published by McGraw-Hill Book Company, Inc. N.Y., Reprinted 1996 by Ignatius Press, San Francisco, pgs. 207, 208) he wrote:

"It is objected that there is much repetition in the Rosary inasmuch as the Lord's Prayer and the Hail Mary are said so often; therefore it is monotonous. That reminds me of a woman who came to see me one evening after instructions. She said, "I would never become a Catholic. You say the same words in the Rosary over and over again, and anyone who repeats the same words is never sincere. I would never believe anyone who repeated his words, and neither would God." I asked her who the man was with her. She said he was her fiancé. I asked: "Does he love you?" "Certainly, he does." "But how do you know?" "He told me." "What did he say?" "He said: 'I love you.' "When did he tell you last?" "About an hour ago." "Did he tell you before?" "Yes, last night." "What did he say?" "I love you." "But never before?" "He tells me every night." I said: "Do not believe him. He is repeating; he is not sincere."

The beautiful truth is that there is no repetition in "I love you." Because there is a new moment of time, another point in space, the words do not mean the same as they did at another time or space. A mother says to her son: "you are a good boy." She may have said it ten thousand times before, but each time it means something different; the whole personality goes out to it anew, as a new historical circumstance summons forth a new outburst of affection. Love is never monotonous in the uniformity of its expression....when we say the Rosary—we are saying to God, the Trinity, to the Incarnate Savior, to the Blessed Mother: "I love you, I love you, I love you." Each time it means something different because, at each decade, our mind is moving to a new demonstration of the Savior's love..."

Each of the Twenty Mysteries gives us new and different insights and reasons to love Our Blessed Lord and Our Blessed Lady.

We don't just tell our loved ones once that we love them. We repeat it and it grows deeper with time. There is great power in repetitious prayer. Each time we say the "Our Father" we deepen in our understanding and love of these words. As we pray them again and again, we unlock new graces and new insights into ourselves and in God. As we repeat each time it has deeper meaning, and we grow deeper in our love of God.

Chapter 4

The Mystery of Meditation

"But Mary kept all these things, pondering them in her heart."
(Lk.2:19)

Using our Imagination to Help our Salvation

The word "meditate" originates in the Latin *meditari* to 'contemplate', to relate to. Meditation is a deep and focused spiritual thinking or pondering, in our hearts and minds, of a Sacred Truth. The ability to meditate varies with each person, however, we can all meditate to some degree. And, we can all do better with a little guidance and practice in the art of meditation. Meditating on the Twenty Mysteries of the Rosary is a great way to have a personal knowledge and encounter with Christ. But, how to meditate is the great challenge. In the Rosary, meditation is remembering, pondering, and applying the mysteries of the Gospel, the examples of Jesus and Mary, and relating them to our daily lives.

The most important thing in meditating on the Rosary is to simply think about or use our minds to imagine the mystery. From this will naturally flow more progressive stages of meditation which involve applying the mystery to our lives, and resolving to do something spiritual as a result of it. There is no need to be discouraged or intimidated by meditation.

First, it is *considering, contemplating, or pondering* the basic Sacred Truth of the Mystery. For instance, when we consider the birth of Christ, the First Christmas and the Third Joyful Mystery, we *imagine* it in front of us. Try to imagine it not as an event centuries old, but as happening now. Imagine yourself transported back in time, and put yourself in the scene. For example, imagine yourself as another person at the foot of the cross or as one of the shepherds at the manger. This first step is the most important. Do not read about the others and get discouraged thinking it is too complicated. If you develop the habit of doing the first step, the others will follow in natural consequence.

Second, we *apply* this Sacred Truth to our own lives. We may consider that Christ was poor, and we are called to the virtue of detachment. This is why at the end of this book each mystery is listed with a spiritual fruit or virtue that we can relate to it. Third, we *resolve* to apply this consideration into an activity, decision, or change to our spiritual life to help us grow closer to Christ. We may decide to review what we own, and try to get rid of unnecessary things that we may like or derive pleasure from, for the purpose of being more attached to God and less to the world. This is why our lord tells us,

"Do not lay up for yourselves treasures on earth, where moth and rust consume and where thieves break in and steal, but lay up for yourselves treasures in heaven, where neither moth nor rust consumes and where thieves do not break in and steal. For where your treasure is, there will your heart be also. Therefore do not be anxious, saying, 'What shall we eat?' or 'What shall we drink?' or 'What shall we wear?' For the Gentiles [Unbelievers] seek all these things; and your heavenly Father knows that you need them all. But seek first his kingdom and his righteousness, and all these things shall be yours as well." (Matt. 6:19-21, 31-33)

The importance of the Mysteries to the Rosary cannot be underestimated, for the mysteries are essential to the Rosary. If we pray the Rosary we must never neglect the mysteries. To pray the Rosary without them is not truly praying the Rosary. The Mysteries complete the fullness of the Rosary's Gospel character. St. Louis De Montfort compares praying the Rosary without the mysteries to having a body without a soul. All it takes is a little effort and a little understanding to integrate true Christian meditation into our prayer life. Once we have broken through the barrier of doubt and fear of meditation, we will find it hard to imagine we may have ever wanted to pray the Rosary without the mysteries. If we do not think about the mysteries, then we are not truly praying the Rosary. We are praying Hail Marys, and they will certainly help us grow, however, to get the full spiritual benefit of the Rosary we cannot omit the mysteries.

Although I've never been to the Pacific Island of Bora Bora, I've seen beautiful pictures of the surf, sand, and palm trees. I've imagined myself on a hammock between two palm trees, drinking a refreshing tropical drink, watching the surf roll in, and feeling the breeze. Since I don't have the money to go there, this is as close as I can get. When I do this I use my imagination and I meditate. We don't have a real time machine to go back to the foot of the cross and be at the crucifixion or the resurrection.

However, God has given us an imagination, and it can be used for good or evil. Our imagination is our spiritual time machine. This is what we do with the Twenty Mysteries of the Holy Rosary, we use our imagination and meditate. We meditate using our imagination, in which we picture the sacred mysteries occurring in detail before us, as if they were actually happening at that moment. We must picture it as if we went back in time, and we are there at that first Christmas night, there at the agony in the garden, and there at the resurrection of Jesus. This is the proper way to meditate on the mysteries of the Rosary. If we have ever seen a movie about the life and passion of Christ that was well done, and we paid attention as we watched it, then we were meditating on the life of Christ. We were meditating on one or more of the Twenty Mysteries of the Rosary. Thinking about the life of Jesus and Mary, that is meditating on the mysteries of the Rosary.

We can use pictures to start our meditation, and use scripture passages to refresh our memories. Did you ever walk into a beautiful Catholic Church and look in awe at the realistic crucifix? Did you stare at the wounds and think about how much Jesus suffered for you? Did you think about how much he loves you, and how little you love him in return? You might not have realized it, but you were meditating on the Fifth Sorrowful Mystery of the Rosary.

Now, combine that deep spiritual thought with the Honor of Mary, His Mother, joining her prayers to yours in the Hail Mary, and you are praying the Rosary. Now you are beginning to understand its beauty and spiritual power to help your soul.

In the Rosary we combine that deep spiritual thought on the crucifixion with the worship of God the Father in the Lord's prayer, the Worship of the Trinity through the Glory Be, and the Honor of Mary his mother, *she who was there* at the foot of the cross. Through praying the Hail Mary, you join your prayers to hers, your heart to hers as you love Jesus with the Immaculate Heart of Mary. In the Rosary you join your contemplation with she whose contemplation of the sufferings of Christ were the most perfect of anyone who ever lived. Do all these things and you are praying the Rosary, the prayer sent by God from heaven.

Pope John Paul II wrote:

"The Rosary, though clearly Marian in character, is at heart a Christocentric prayer. In the sobriety of its elements, it has all the depth of the Gospel message in its entirety, of which it can be said to be a compendium. ...With the Rosary, the Christian people sits at the school of Mary and is led to contemplate the beauty of the face of Christ and to experience the depths of his love. Through the Rosary the faithful receive abundant grace, as though from the very hands of the Mother of the Redeemer... Against the background of the words Ave Maria the principal events of the life of Jesus Christ pass before the eyes of the soul. They take shape in the complete series of the joyful, sorrowful, and glorious mysteries, and they put us in living communion with Jesus through—we might say—the heart of his Mother." (Rosarium Virginis Mariae)

The Rosary helps us to love Jesus with the Heart of Mary

Did you ever think about the first Christmas? What was it like to stand in front of the manger and look at the baby Jesus? To think that the King of the Universe loved you so much he came down from heaven as a poor child. He who had all things became a man who had nothing, to be an example for us not to be too attached to this world—to be rather attracted by the riches of virtue and goodness. Did you think, "Maybe I should be more like Christ, and be more detached from this world." If you did this you were meditating on the Third Joyful Mystery of the Rosary: the Nativity. See how easy it is? Meditating should not be intimidating!

Did you ever think about the miracle of the first Mass? Did you think about how Jesus gave us his body and blood in the Eucharist and how it is present in all the tabernacles of the world? And, how he prepared his disciples for his new mysterious presence on earth? Also, how the first Mass was the way he would begin his passion, death, and resurrection? And, that he would make himself be even closer to us by receiving His body, blood, soul, and divinity through Holy Communion? Did you consider how important this was, that he saved it to be his last miracle, his last action before he began his passion in the Garden of Gethsemani? If you thought about it, then you meditated on the Fifth Mystery of Light.

Scripture says: "*I will meditate on all thy work, and muse on thy mighty deeds.*" (Ps 77:12). We meditate on the Mysteries of the Rosary by using our imagination to picture each event in the life of Jesus and Mary, occurring in front of us as we say the Hail Mary prayers. Because it is so difficult to concentrate on two things at once, I often pause for a moment, when I think of the mystery I am doing and simply meditate upon it—or think about it before I continue with the Hail Marys. I have found it is best to meditate at the beginning of each decade and then pray with the meditation fresh in mind. Do not let meditation scare you. Try it and you will find it won't take long to get used to it.

Meditating on the life, words, and deeds of the Lord is a joy, and a way to union with Christ.

"Oh, how I have loved your law, O Lord! It is my meditation all the day. Through your commandment you have made me wiser than my enemies: for it is ever with me. I have understood more than all my teachers because your testimonies are my meditation." (Ps.119:97-99)

The mysteries show the depths of the Rosary as a prayer suitable for spiritual beginners and advanced. The contemplative aspect of the Twenty Mysteries is virtually inexhaustible. The mysteries add a dimension which makes this prayer unlike any other. It is even designed to help us deal with out natural inclination toward distraction by giving us a second object of concentration, besides the words of our prayers, namely the life of Jesus and Mary. The more we meditate and think about their lives, the more we love them and grow in grace and understanding of the Gospel. Meditating on the sorrowful mysteries is especially beneficial since we see in them how concrete God's love for us truly is. In meditation on the mysteries of the rosary, day after day we see Christ born, suffer, die for our sins, and then be raised from the dead. These meditations give us an increasing knowledge and love of God with each new day. They gain a steady spiritual progress for our souls. Through these meditations everyday we renew in our hearts the incarnation, the crucifixion, the resurrection of Christ, and the final reward of Mary's Crowning. In this way the Gospel becomes a daily event in our lives as we recall, again and again, with ever deepening love and understanding, how great his love for us really was. This is why God loves for us to pray the Rosary so much, so that we can really see and experience his love for us.

The Rosary meditations cultivate knowledge and love of Jesus and Mary. They give the strength to suffer and follow their example and virtues. It makes the soul's knowledge of Christ's passion more intense and heartfelt, aiding in our spiritual union with him. The life of Christ can and should be the center of our life. This can be done through meditation on the life of Christ, especially in the joyful, luminous, sorrowful, and glorious mysteries of the Rosary. When we meditate and imagine him suffering in front of us, as in the sorrowful mysteries, we are more united with him. Through the knowledge and understanding we receive of Jesus suffering, in a sense we experience his suffering through meditation. It is as if we are suffering with him when we picture his sufferings in our imagination. This is because through our faith we are one with him, so that what is done to him is done to us and what is done to us is done to him (Mt.25:40).

The Rosary is the Door to Contemplation

The Rosary is a combination of vocal prayer (mainly the Our Father and Hail Mary) and mental prayer (the meditations on the mysteries of the life of Jesus and Mary). When we are praying in a group we would say the prayers of the Rosary out loud, but if we are by ourselves we normally pray these prayers silently in our mind. This is similar to the meditation which occurs silently in our minds without any vocal sounds. I believe that these vocal prayers, said internally and joined to meditation, become the door to contemplation. On vocal prayer, meditation, and contemplation the Catechism teaches us:

The Christian Tradition comprises three major expressions of the life of prayer: vocal, meditation, and contemplative prayer. They have in common the recollection of the heart.

Vocal prayer, founded on the union of body and soul in human nature, associates the body with the interior prayer of the heart, following Christ's example of praying to his Father and teaching the Our Father to his disciples.

Through his Word, God speaks to man. By words, mental or vocal, our prayer takes flesh. Yet it is most important that the heart should be present to him to whom we are speaking in prayer: "Whether or not our prayer is heard depends not on the number of words, but on the fervor of our souls."

Vocal prayer is an essential element of the Christian life. To his disciples, drawn by their Master's silent prayer, **Jesus teaches a vocal prayer, the Our Father.**

Because it is external and so thoroughly human, vocal prayer is the form of prayer most readily accessible to groups. Even interior prayer, however, cannot neglect vocal prayer. Prayer is internalized to the extent that we become aware of him "to whom we speak." **Thus vocal prayer becomes an initial form of contemplative prayer.**

What is contemplative prayer? St. Teresa answers: "Contemplative prayer in my opinion is nothing else than a close sharing between friends; it means taking time frequently to be alone with him who we know loves us."

Contemplative prayer is a gaze of faith, fixed on Jesus... **Contemplation also turns its gaze on the mysteries of the life of Christ.** Thus it learns the "interior knowledge of our Lord," the more to love him and follow him.

Meditation engages thought, imagination, emotion, and desire. This mobilization of faculties is necessary in order to deepen our convictions of faith, prompt the conversion of our heart, and strengthen our will to follow Christ. **Christian prayer tries above all to meditate on the mysteries of Christ, as in** *lectio divina* or **the rosary.**" (Catechism of the Catholic Church: 2721, 2722, 2700, 2701, 2704, 2709, 2715, 2708) [Bold type in the above quotation is my emphasis].

The Seven Main Qualities of Prayer

1. **Devotion**: Putting our hearts into our prayers. *"This people honors me with their lips, but their heart is far from me."* (Mt.15:18)

2. **Fervor**: An intense desire to serve God. *"And being in agony he prayed more earnestly; and his sweat became like great drops of blood falling down upon the ground."* (Lk.22:44)

3. **Perseverance**: *"And he told them a parable, to the effect that they ought always to pray and not lose heart. He said, 'In a certain city there was a judge who neither feared God nor regarded man; and there was a widow in that city who kept coming to him and saying, 'vindicate me against my adversary.' For a while he refused; but afterward he said to himself, 'Though I neither fear God nor regard man, yet because this widow bothers me, I will vindicate her, or she will wear me out by her continual coming.' And the Lord said, 'Hear what the unrighteous judge says: And will not God vindicate his elect, who cry to him day and night? Will he delay long over them? I tell you, he will vindicate them speedily."* (Lk.18:1-8, Lk.11:5-10, Matt.24:13)

When we pray for another person we need to remember God's respect for free will. We are not robots or computers, we are human beings who freely choose to love or hate God. God does not force us or program us to love Him, because love is not love unless it is freely chosen.

I once spoke to a young girl who told me she didn't believe in God. I asked her why and she said she prayed for her dad to come back to her mom and he didn't do it. So she didn't believe in God. I tried to explain to her that God can send graces to do the right thing, but men still have a free will to chose not to. God sends grace, but he does not take free will. I told her about St.Monica who prayed for 30 years for her son St. Augustine, and how God finally rewarded her prayer with her son becoming one of the greatest saints in history. If she didn't persevere, many souls who were helped by her son's writings and example might never have been saved. When we pray for people, especially family members, we need to recognize that God must work with free will, and he never forces love.

4. **Humility**: *"God opposes the proud, but gives grace to the humble. Submit yourselves therefore to God."* (Jam.4:6) *"...for everyone who exalts himself will be humbled, but he who humbles himself will be exalted."* (Lk.18:9-14) (Matt.6:1-6)

5. **Attention**: How can we expect God to listen to our prayer, if we are not paying attention to it? (Matt.6:7,8) Involuntary distractions in prayer are inevitable, but we should try to minimize them.

6. **Faith**: *"He who trusts in the Lord is safe."* (Prv.29:25) *"Those who trust in you cannot be put to shame."* (Dan.3:40) *"With men this is impossible, but with God all things are possible."* (Mat.19:26), *"For with God nothing will be impossible."* (Lk.1:37) *"Without faith it is impossible to please him."* (Heb.11:6)

7. **Right Priority**: When we pray we need to have the right priority, namely that of God's will over our own (Lk.22:42, Mt.6:31-33, 16:26). Does God always answer our prayers? **Yes**. There are three answers to prayer—yes, no, and please wait. No prayer is unanswered, and no prayer is unheard.

God grants us in prayer only those things which work for our salvation. There are times I asked God for things in prayer and I was later grateful He said, "no". I later received information which I originally did not have when I was praying for this. We need to remember that if God says no to our prayer, we are to still trust in his wisdom and loving providence. He knows more than we do, and at times we are called to the cross, to be tested, and to endure hardships we would not choose on our own. God will grant us what we ask for, even if it is a luxury or a convenience, if he can do so within the individual plan of salvation he has for us. We must always have the right priority in prayer, because our heavenly Father knows what is best for us—better than we do. Whatever we want for ourselves on earth, must be secondary to salvation.

"If you, evil as you are, know how to give good gifts to your children, how much more will your heavenly Father give the Good Spirit to those who ask him!" (Lk.11:13). "Draw near to God, and he will draw near to you." (Jam.4:8) "Behold, I stand at the door and knock. If any man listens to my voice and opens the door to me, I will come in to him and will sup with him, and he with me." (Rev.3:20)

We have our list of things we want in prayer, and God has his list of things he wants from us. He wants us to get to heaven, he wants us to get away from sin, he wants us to be purified from our attachments to sin and this world, and he wants us to do penance and reparation for sin. So whenever we pray we must be humble and submissive to God's will, God's plan, and his providence. When we pray the Lord's prayer we pray, *"Thy will be done on earth as it is in heaven."* —not, "My will be done on earth, as it should be in heaven!" We are not God, we are not in charge. We are creatures created by God. We are on earth to be tested by God, to labor for God to learn from God, to suffer for God, and to prepare to reign with God in heaven. If we don't always get what we want in prayer, we need to keep this in mind. This world is temporary, it is a place of preparation for our place in eternity. We are not here to rule, we are here to work. We must join in Christ's prayer, in the agony in the garden, *"Father if it is possible let this cup of suffering pass from me, yet not my will, but thine be done."*

When we receive a "no" from God in answer to a prayer, it touches on the problem of evil. The problem of evil, simply stated, is: "If God is all good, then why does he allow evil?" The short answer is God only allows evil that he may bring a greater good out of it. The evils we suffer in this life are temporary, the rewards we get in the next life are permanent. This life is a place where we are put to a great test between good and evil, and if we choose good we will receive a greater reward in heaven which would never have been possible for us had we not undergone the unique test of this life. God allows evil that good men may conquer it, *"Overcome evil with good."* (Rom.12:21)

God allows evil to give us a means to a greater reward and enable us to unite our suffering to Christ as penance for sins. *"He who overcomes, I will permit him to sit with me upon my throne; as I also have overcome and have sat with my Father on his throne."* (Rev.3:21, Job.42:10, 12.)

We do not fully understand how this can be and that is itself part of the test; however, we must understand that this world is a world which plays out the battle between good and evil. It preserves the good of free will and allows serious choices between good and evil which involve serious consequences and serious responsibilities. Through the great evil of the crucifixion—the murder of the sinless Son of God—God brought about the great good of redemption: salvation for the world.

"Did not the Christ have to suffer these things before entering into his glory?" (Lk.24:26) Do not we have to suffer before sharing in his glory? "Through his suffering, my servant shall justify many...he shall take away the sins of many, and win pardon for their offenses." (Is.53:11, 12)

This then is the test of life: Do we, the creatures of this world, sit in judgement on the judge and creator of the world, and convict him of evil because we don't want to follow him in carrying the cross? And, do we then join in the evil ourselves through sinning against God and our neighbor? Or, do we recognize man as the cause of evil through his wrong choices and join in the creator's efforts to reverse the evils of the world through grace, through prayer, and obedience to his commandments. Do we wish to be hypocrites who do evil and blame God for it, or do we wish to be honest about ourselves and the test of this life and admit our sinfulness, seek forgiveness, and repent of our evils? Think of the pride and foolishness of those who say, "If there is a God, he's not a good God. I know better than God. If I were God, I would be a better God. I would eliminate all pain and suffering." God will eliminate all pain and suffering, for those who choose good over evil, for those who deserve it. Those who choose evil over good, and hurt the innocent, have abused the good of free will and shall not be given another chance to do so in eternity.

There are certain things that God will give us whether we ask for them or not, but there are certain things that God will only give to us if we ask for them in prayer. From the smallest request to the greatest, God wants us to speak to him and to ask Him to help us. If God answers our prayer request with a yes, it will help us grow in faith. If God answers our prayer request with a "no" or a "please wait", then it is time for us to prove our love and endure victoriously the test of our faith. We should never stop praying because God did not grant our request the way we wanted, because the primary purpose of prayer is salvation and everything else is secondary.

It is through prayer that we prepare daily to spend eternity with the Father who created us, the Father who gave his only beloved Son on the cross for us, and the Father who sends His Holy Spirit to live within our souls forever. We should pray at least 5 to 15 minutes everyday. Since God is the most important "person" in our life, we should speak to Him everyday. We spend far more time each day pursuing recreation, than we do in strengthening our relationship with God. Our spiritual life is the priority. And, God is certainly more important than anyone or anything else in our life. He deserves a priority of time, *"pray always"* (Lk.18:1, 1 Thess. 5:17, Eph. 6:18).

The Rosary is the Answer

Chapter 5

What to Pray: The Word of God versus the Word of Man

"And in praying do not heap up empty phrases as the Gentiles do; for they think that they will be heard for their many words. Do not be like them, for your Father knows what you need before you ask him. **Pray then like this:** *Our Father who art in heaven..."* (Mt.6:7-9)

Pray Like This—Our Father...

In choosing what prayers to pray Our Lady's simple words of obedience help point the way: *"His mother said to the servants, Do whatever He tells you."* (John 2:5) Obviously the best prayer at any given time depends on God's will so it could be formal or spontaneous; however, as a general rule formal prayer should be our *foundational* prayer—the source from which spontaneous prayer springs.

We cannot substitute prayer in our words for formal prayers in God's word. No matter how smart we are, even if we have three Ph.D.s, we are not smarter than God. No matter how good we are, we are not better than God. So how can we trust prayers in our own words, built on our own weakened wills and darkened intellect to be better than the word of God? It's revealed by God to us to be prayed by us. If our prayer life has no formal prayer based on God's word it is deficient. Our prayer to God in our own words is to be built upon a disciplined prayer based in God's word. *"Unless the Lord builds the house, those who build it labor in vain."* (Ps.127:1) *"Every one then who hears these words of mine and does them will be like a wise man who built his house upon the rock."* (Mt.7:24) Our soul is our spiritual house. The foundation of our spiritual life is prayer, and that prayer form which is our foundation must be the Word of God.

The many approved apparitions of Mary involving the Rosary, Lourdes, Fatima, etc... show the approval and design of our Heavenly Father in the Rosary. In praying the rosary we do not pray the word of man, we pray the word of God.

True prayer is the word of God in action. God gives His word to us, we accept it, believe it, say it, and pray it—over and over again. This generates the grace of God for our souls through the word of God in our souls.

Many times people say,"O yes, I pray." However, that means a few lines to God in their own words about what they want, not a disciplined formal prayer life based on God's word. We are to speak to God all day in our own words, but this is more the practice of the presence of God than our true daily foundational prayer.

In quoting St.Thomas Aquinas the Catechism of the Catholic Church says:

"The Lord's Prayer is the most perfect of prayers...In it we ask, not only for all the things we can rightly desire, but also in the sequence that they should be desired. This prayer not only teaches us to ask for things, but also in what order we should desire them." (CCC2763)

Reinforcing the importance of the Our Father and Hail Mary we hear St.Teresa of Avila, one of the few female Doctors of the Church, saying:

"...'the Our Father and the Hail Mary are sufficient.' This last statement, Sisters, I agree with. And indeed they are sufficient! It is always good to base your prayer on prayers coming from the mouth of the Lord. In this matter those who warn us are right, for if our nature were not so weak and our devotion so lukewarm there wouldn't be any need to compose other prayers, nor would there be need for other books." (*The Collected Works of St. Teresa of Avila*, Vol. 2, ICS Publications, Institute of Carmelite Studies, Washington D.C., 1980, Translated by Kieran Kavanaugh, O.C.D. and Otilio Rodriguez, O.D.C., pg.118)

Our words are not better than God's word. God's word lifts us up and guides us specifically the way we need it. "*Thy will be done on earth as it is in heaven.*" (Mt.6:10) "*My Father, if it be possible, let this cup pass from me; nevertheless, not as I will, but as thou wilt.*" (Mt.26:39) We are sinners, we are weak, we need healing, we need guidance. God is perfect, he is the spiritual doctor of our souls, the divine physician. He is the designer and creator of our souls, and the designer and creator of prayers specifically for our souls. He knows what we need before we ask, and what we need, but forget to ask for. Many don't want to pray God's word, they feel it is too restrictive. They want to make prayer and God in their own image. Scripture says, "*enter by the narrow gate...*"(Mt.7:13). Prayer is not just about what we need, "petition". It is also about adoration, worship, thanksgiving—the other three of the Four Main Purposes of prayer. Does our prayer in our own words include these things? I do not say don't pray to God in your own words. I pray to God in my own words and encourage others to do so. I say do not let that be your only prayer, pray to God in the words he gave us to pray as well.

Pray to God in the words he custom designed for our souls to get us to heaven. He made the prayers to save our souls, to strengthen and guide them to heaven. God's words do not come from a weak human filled with sins, they are perfect and are designed to make us perfect. *"You, therefore, must be perfect as your heavenly Father is perfect."* (Mt.5:48) I would not be so confident to think my prayer in my words were better for my soul than God's Prayer in God's word which he designed personally for my soul, and that of every soul he created.

The more we pray the Our Father and the Hail Mary, the more God's words become our words: the more does our heart become like his Heart, the more does our thoughts become like his thoughts, and the more our soul reflects and possesses His Holy Spirit. *"For out of the abundance of the heart the mouth speaks...I tell you, on the day of judgment men will render account for every careless word they utter; for by your words you will be justified, and by your words you will be condemned."* (Mt.12:34, 36, 37) Let us therefore pray as Jesus taught us, and make our heart like his.

Spontaneous prayers to God in our own words will be more fruitful if they are based on a solid, disciplined foundation of formal prayer in God's word. Formal prayer is not to stifle spontaneous prayer, but to compliment and prepare us for spontaneous prayer. A good spontaneous prayer is a prayer in our own words expressing our hearts to God, with the help of the Holy Spirit within.

The Rosary is the prayer that worships the Father, Honors, the Mother, and meditates on the Gospel: the life of Christ and his Mother. The Rosary is the true Gospel prayer, it is the Gospel alive in our souls. The Rosary is so spiritually perfect and complete that the mother of God came from heaven to tell us the Father has given his approval!

Why strain ourselves trying to emulate the Our Father and the Hail Mary in our own words? Why not be humble enough to take God's words over ours and make his words our words? God wishes us to pray to him in our own words in *addition* to praying to him in His words.

However, you who insist on choosing your own words *instead* of God's words—I ask you—did you remember to honor his name? "hallowed be thy name". Did you remember to put His will over yours: "Thy will be done on earth as it is in heaven." You will be doing so much over if you try to do it right. Why not simply use his words instead of trying to imitate them or match them?

Why should we pray in God's word? Because he who said, "thou shalt not commit adultery," also said, "Pray that you may not enter into temptation, the spirit is willing, but the flesh is weak." O Lord, how should we pray not to enter into temptation? Our Lord says, *"Pray then like this: Our Father who art in heaven..."* (Mt.6:7-9)

The same God who gave us the ten commandments also gave us the means to keep them. He gave us the "Our Father" and the "Hail Mary", he gave us baptism, the Eucharist, and he gave us His words to be studied, prayed, and lived. What should we pray, the word of God or the word of man? Do we pray God's word or our words? Our conflict is resolved. We pray the word of God as our primary prayer, then we pray to God in our own words inspired and based upon His.

A Commentary on the "Our Father"

The first line is, "Our Father who art in heaven." In the beginning of the Lord's Prayer we find the first words tell us not only who we are praying to—God; but, what our relationship is with Him, namely—that He is our Father. So, in the first two words we know who we are as well. If he is Our Father then we are his sons and daughters. This also corresponds to the first commandment, to not have any false gods before him. It establishes Him as our God and Father in heaven.

The second line, "Hallowed be thy name" corresponds to the second commandment, namely, *"You shall not take the name of the Lord your God in vain."* (Ex.20:7) Interestingly enough, this is the only commandment that tells us we have no excuse for breaking it, *"The Lord will not hold him guiltless who takes his name in vain."* (Ex.20:7) This commandment is often broken by men with little thought, yet it betrays an inner spiritual illness and distance from God. To counter this illness the divine physician has us make our first act in prayer, after we have established who we are praying to, to be honoring His name. Thus we have the Lord's Prayer beginning not with petition, requesting for what we want or need, but with worship and adoration of the holy name of God.

"*Thy kingdom come, thy will be done, on earth, as it is in heaven.*" This line shows that after identifying God as our Father and honoring his name, we seek his will over ours. In this line we seek to extend the love of heaven onto the spiritual battlefield of earth, by doing his will. When we do his will on earth, it will lead us to heaven. The Father in heaven will be with us on earth, and it will lead us to be with him in heaven. We bring the love, the goodness, and the kindness of heaven to earth when we keep the ten commandments and the works of mercy. Conversely, when we sin we bring the hatred and evil of hell to the earth. The hearts of men are the conduits of heaven and hell. We decide which gate to open with our free will.

Christ's prayer in the agony of the Garden compliments this line, "Father if it is possible let this cup [of suffering] pass from me, yet not my will but thine be done." (Mt.26:39) And what is His will? We know what his will is, it is the keeping of the Ten Commandments, the performing of the seven physical and seven spiritual works of mercy, and the worthy reception of the sacraments. In this line we are asking the Lord to help us keep His commandments for they indeed are his will for us on earth. It is interesting to note how the first two lines of the Lord's prayer, correspond to the first two commandments, and how the third corresponds to them all— "Thy will be done..." (Mt.6:10). "Give us this day our daily bread." In this our first petition, we ask for physical needs (daily food, shelter, etc.) and spiritual needs, namely the Eucharist, the "*Living bread come down from heaven.*" (Jn.6:51) "*They recognized him in the breaking of the bread.*" (Lk24:30, 31) The previous verse concerns primarily the commandments; this line concerns the sacraments, primarily the Eucharist.

"*Forgive us our trespasses as we forgive those who trespass against us.*" In this petition we seek contrition for our sins, through humbly asking for forgiveness. Our Lord connects his forgiveness to ours when he asks us to humbly let go of any grudges or anger in our hearts for times when our neighbor has failed to love us as we have failed to love God. This line concerns the fourteen works of mercy, but primarily the one which says, "forgive all injuries."

"*Lead us not into temptation.*" In this we ask for strength in the time of temptation, as our Lord said:

"The spirt is willing but the flesh is weak, pray that you may not enter into temptation." (Mt. 27:41) "Let no one say when he is tempted, 'I am tempted by God'; for God cannot be tempted with evil and he himself tempts no one; but each person is tempted when he is lured and enticed by his own desire. Then desire when it has conceived gives birth to sin; and sin when it is full-grown brings forth death....Resist the devil and he will flee from you. Draw near to God and he will draw near to you." (Jam. 1:13-15, 4:7, 8) In Genesis God counsels Cain to resist temptation before he kills his brother saying, "If you do well, will you not be accepted? And if you do not do well, sin is couching at the door; its desire is for you, but you must master it." (Gen.4:1)

"Deliver us from evil." This is asking for protection by Our Lord from physical evils and spiritual evils. But, most of all deliverance from the greatest evil, namely sin and from its author namely—the evil one, the devil. Sin is the opposite of what we ask for at the beginning, namely *"Thy will be done."* When we do his will we are delivered from evil, and brought into grace.

In commenting on prayer and the "Our Father" Blessed Mother Teresa of Calcutta said:

"Prayer, to be fruitful, must come from the heart...Jesus taught his disciples to pray. Call God your Father; praise and glorify his name. Do his will as the saints do in heaven; ask for daily bread, spiritual and temporal; ask for forgiveness of your own sins and that you may forgive others, and also for the grace not to give in to temptations and for the final grace to be delivered from the evil that is in us and around us...Love to pray, feel the need to pray often during the day, and take the trouble to pray. If you want to pray better, you must pray more. Prayer enlarges the heart until it is capable of containing God's gift of himself...For us religious, prayer is a sacred duty and sublime mission. Conscious of the many urgent needs and interests we carry in our hands, we will ascend the altar of prayer, take up our rosary..." (*Jesus the Word to be Spoken,* Mother Teresa, Servant Books, Ann Arbor, Michigan, pg3, 6, 8)

A Commentary on the "Hail Mary"

The grace of God to pray the Rosary is a great gift, not to be neglected or taken for granted. In the *Hail Mary* are the first words, the very cornerstone, of the Gospel of Jesus Christ. In his great book True Devotion to Mary, St. Louis De Montfort told us: "Just as the salvation of the world began with the Hail Mary, so the salvation of each individual is bound up with it." (*God Alone,* Montfort Publications, Bay Shore, N.Y., 1995, pg. 369.) The Hail Mary is the great prayer God has given us to worship Him, to honor his Mother, and to gain her prayers and God's grace for our soul.

"*Hail Mary*" This starts the Gospel and the message of Salvation for the world. These words are given by God the Father to the Archangel Gabriel to express in God's own words, the honor due to Mary as the Mother of God the Son, the spouse of the Holy Spirit, and the one faithful Daughter of the Eternal Father. When we repeat these words in honor of Mary, first given by our Father in heaven, we join in the honor given to Mary by God and the Angels. When we say these words we honor her as God honors her, and then He blesses us because we share in His will.

"*Full of grace, the Lord is with thee*" In these words we proclaim her sinlessness and her unique union with God. Mary is full of grace, because at her Immaculate Conception she was given the grace of God and it never left her. She is full of grace, and empty of sin. The Lord is with her because He created her to be the Mother of His son and the Mother of "*all those who keep the commandments and give witness to Jesus.*" (Rev.12:17) She is our heavenly Mother, and her job is to protect us from sin, and make us like her firstborn Son, Jesus Christ. The God of grace, named her through the angel, "*full of grace*", and the Lord pronounced to all generations that he is with her—forever!

"*Blessed art thou among women, and blessed is the fruit of thy womb Jesus.*" This shows her special relationship to all humanity and her role above all but her son. Jesus was blessed among men, and Mary was blessed among women. Mary has replaced Eve, as the *New Woman* created by God, the first woman of the new Heavenly Garden of Eden. Mary is the new "*Mother of all the Living*" (Gen.3:20) who are alive in Christ (Rev.12:17). Mary is first among women because she is the Mother of God, and the most faithful of all the servants of God. Because of her humility and faithfulness, she received a special place in God's creation. And, Mary spoke through the Holy Spirit in a prophetic foreshadowing of these words that would be repeated so often in the Rosary through the centuries. "For behold, *henceforth all generations will call me blessed; for he who is mighty has done great things for me.*" (Lk.1:48, 49) Speaking through St. Elizabeth the Holy Spirit gives us these words, which bless

Mary, and the fruit of her womb, Jesus. In every Hail Mary, we say the Holy Name of Jesus, and we bless it as the Holy Spirit did, indicating the cause and source of all blessedness.

"*Holy Mary, Mother of God*" In this we recognize the Holiness of Mary, and that she is the Mother of God. This unique title places her above all angels and saints in heaven.

"*Pray for us sinners, now and at the hour of our death.*" Here we petition the prayers of this great woman of God, whom he has chosen to place above us in the order of grace and honor, to be our spiritual mother. We gain her prayers at that moment— "*now*", and they are joined to ours raising the value of our prayers in the sight of God, because we have sinned against God and she has not. So, the prayers of "*us sinners*" are joined to the prayers of the one whom God has said is "*full of Grace,*" and "*The Lord is with thee.*" And, the prayer of the sinner is joined to the prayer of the just, and they are magnified in the sight of God, because he loves her so much. Though he might refuse us sinners, he will not refuse her whom he chose to be His Mother. For this is the mystery of Mary in God's plan of salvation, that she is our spiritual helpmate, our divinely appointed mother, helping and guiding her children home to heaven, to our Father's house. Her prayers are like a heavenly amplifier that raises the power of grace in our petitions to the almighty.

This great prayer given by God yields a triple blessing each time we say it. First, it gains worship for God and honor for Mary. Second, it gains the prayers of the greatest saint in heaven joined to us sinners on earth. Third, it gains for us one more prayer from Mary. She returns again to pray for us at that most crucial moment known only to God, "*the hour of our death*". This moment is the last chance the devil has to steal our souls from heaven. This prayer is perhaps the best eternal fire insurance available under heaven. Our heavenly mother who loves her children with a mighty protective vengeance will be there for her faithful sons and daughters at the end of their lives. For those who were faithful to honor her during their lives will receive the final blessing of the *Hail Mary* prayer. She will manifest through the grace of God, a powerful final display of her love for us during our last day and hour on earth. She will do this to protect us from mortal sin, and either keep us in grace or bring us to grace, so that we can join her in heaven, eternally loving our Heavenly Father! "AMEN"! "Alleluia!" Thank you God the Father for giving us so wonderful a Mother, and so great a gift and grace through Mary, the First

Lady of Heaven.

The Rosary is the Psalter of Jesus and Mary

In the parish where I am pastor, we have begun the practice of ending the general intercessions at all masses with a Hail Mary. At the end of the intercessions I say, "Let us join our prayers on earth with those of our spiritual Mother in heaven, Hail Mary...." I know there are many parishes which already do this, and it is my hope that this practice of praying the Hail Mary at the end of the intercessions will eventually become universal liturgical law! Since the Lord's Prayer is already part of every mass, I believe it is pleasing to the Father that the Hail Mary be part of the mass as well.

As the Rosary is the Psalter of Jesus and Mary, so too is the 150 Psalms the Psalter of David. When we pray the Psalms of the Old Testament, or the Psalter of David, we are also praying the word of God. The variety of words in the 150 Psalms, are often found to be easier to pray than the Rosary for some people because of the variety of words. The Rosary can be hard to pray for some people, especially in the beginning, because of the distractions which come easier due to the repetition. We should not, however, give up because of the challenge to our nature. We should seek to embrace the supernatural character of the Rosary and its great benefits. We seek to receive its benefits, therefore, we should accept the spiritual labor and challenge involved in repetitious prayer. St. Louis De Montfort writes:

"Since simple and uneducated people are not able to say the Psalms of David, the Rosary is held to be just as fruitful for them as David's Psalter is for others.

"But the Rosary can be considered to be even more valuable than the latter for three reasons:

1. Firstly, because the Angelic Psalter bears a nobler fruit, that of the Word Incarnate, whereas David's Psalter only prophesies His coming;
2. Secondly, just as the real thing is more important than its prefiguration and as the body is more than its shadow, in the same way the Psalter of Our Lady is greater than David's Psalter which did no more than prefigure it;
3. And thirdly, because Our Lady's Psalter or the Rosary (made up of the Our Father and Hail Mary) is the direct work of the Most Blessed

Trinity and was not made through a human instrument."
(*The Secret of the Rosary*, by St. Louis Mary De Montfort, Montfort Publications, Bay Shore, N.Y. 11706 , pg.25)

A large portion of the Divine Office contains Psalms from David's Psalter. The Divine Office or The Liturgy of the Hours is the official prayer of the Church. It is a beautiful prayer that comes to us from the scriptures and tradition of the church. This is the Church's response to the Lord's request to "*pray always*" (Lk.18:1, 21:36, 1Thes.5:17). This is why the prayers are divided into the different "hours" or time periods of the day, primarily, morning, noon, evening, and night. Scripture says: "*Seven times a day I praise thee for thy righteous ordinances.*" (Psalms 119:164), "*Peter and John were going up to the temple at the hour of prayer...*" (Acts 3:1), "*And he told them a parable, to the effect that they ought always to pray and not lose heart.*" (Lk.18:1)

The 150 Old Testament Psalms of David or David's Psalter, is the heart of the Divine Office, but it also includes the Our Father, the Hail Mary, other new testament prayers such as the Canticle of Zachariah (Lk.1:68-79), and the Magnificat (Lk.1:46-55), the prayer of Mary.

The Rosary is easier to learn than the Liturgy of the Hours and easier to carry than a prayer book. The Rosary has a greater simplicity and mobility than the Liturgy of the Hours, but each has its own beauty and value. The Rosary is simply easier to pray in places where reading from a prayer book is simply not practical or convenient. Also, some people find the complex page flipping in the Divine Office to be difficult, while others find the variety of words in the Psalms and prayers of the office desirable. The time and place, the personality of the individual, and their obligations, can help determine the most appropriate prayer. Many people, especially clergy and religious, pray both the Liturgy of the Hours and the Holy Rosary. I find both prayers are beautiful, and each has its own advantages.

The Church sees the value of the Rosary officially in its code of canon law. The Rosary is to be prayed by seminarians preparing for the priesthood. Canon 246.3

"Devotion to the Blessed Virgin Mary, including the rosary, mental prayer and other exercises of piety are to be fostered, so that the students may acquire the spirit of prayer and be strengthened in their vocation." Also, it is to be prayed by religious. Canon 663.4 says, "They are to have a special devotion to the Virgin Mother of God, the example and protectress of all consecrated life, including

by way of the rosary."
(*The Code of Canon Law, In English Translation*, pgs.41, 120, copyright 1983, The Canon Law Society Trust, Collins Liturgical Publications, Distributed in the United States of America by William B. Eerdmans Publishing Company, 225 Jefferson Ave., S.E.Grand Rapids, MI)

The Prayer of Aspiration

In addition to the Liturgy of the Hours, and the Holy Rosary, there are also prayers of aspiration. All three of these prayer forms are either based directly on God's word, related to it, or come from some heavenly apparition. I have found myself with short moments of time where I didn't have the energy or concentration to even say a "Hail Mary". In these instances it is best to pray one of the prayers of aspiration. When I was in the hospital, recovering from surgery and going in and out of consciousness I simply prayed some prayers of aspiration. When I had recovered enough I returned to the Rosary, but we may find ourselves at times with short moments, or under great duress where we can't even concentrate well enough to pray the Our Father or Hail Mary. If you are extremely tired, fatigued, or short on time, the prayer of aspiration is a nice niche filler.

The Prayer of Aspiration is a short formal prayer of a few words. It expresses faith, petition, or charity. It comes from the Latin word *Aspirare*, which literally means, to breathe upon. It is expressed in very select wording and often is poetic. It's purpose is to help someone maintain a spirit of recollection, a remembrance of the presence of God, during the busy day.

First, let us look at the prayers of aspiration found in scripture. In the parable of the Pharisee and the Tax Collector we read of an example of repetitious prayer in the form of aspiration: "*But the tax collector...beat his breast, saying 'God, be merciful to me a sinner!' I tell you, this man went down to his house justified...*" (Lk.18:14) This is an example of the prayer of Aspiration. Jesus in the Garden prayed, "*Father, if thou art willing, remove this cup from me; nevertheless not my will, but thine, be done.*" (Lk.22:42). Also, St. Thomas the Apostle prayed to the Risen Christ, "*My Lord and My God!*" (Jn.20:28).

The Kyrie and the Responsorial Psalm at Mass are also a form of the prayer of Aspiration. In tradition we also find many examples of this prayer.

St. Francis of Assisi once spent the whole night in prayer, repeating the aspiration, *"My God and My All."* Other traditional examples are a simple reverent repeating of the word, *"Father"* or the Holy Name of *"Jesus"*, or *"Jesus, I love you."* Others include, *"Glory to the Father, and to the Son and to the Holy Spirit." "Jesus, meek and humble of heart, make my heart like yours."*

Some of my favorites are: *"Sacred Heart of Jesus, have mercy on us."* (From the Litany of the Sacred Heart), "Immaculate Heart of Mary, pray for us", (From the words of Our Lady, given as part of the Green Scapular Apparition), *"We adore you O Christ, and we bless you: because by your holy cross you have redeemed the world."* (from the Stations of the Cross), *"For the sake of His sorrowful passion, have mercy on us and on the whole world."* (From the Mercy Apparitions), and my all time favorite which I pray before I start my Rosary, *"O Mary Conceived without sin, pray for us who have recourse to thee "*, (from the Apparition of the Miraculous Medal, 1830). Many of these prayers are found in the Handbook of Indulgences and are connected to Indulgences. It is a common practice of the saints to use these short prayers, and all of us by virtue of our baptism are called to be saints. These prayers are an easy way of maintaining a consciousness of God and his eternal truths, and of remembering we are always in his glorious presence.

Properly Understanding Luke 11:27, 28

Unfortunately, some ill-informed people use misinterpretations of scripture to attack the Holy Rosary, and I wish to address this issue. The passage in Luke Chapter Eleven is the one most misused to attack devotion to Mary. In order to be thoroughly scriptural I must confront this directly.

Some have misinterpreted Luke 11:27,28 as being a verse which speaks against the Hail Mary prayer, this is another example of how scripture can be misquoted. The devil misquoted scripture as a way to trip up Jesus in the temptation (Lk.4:9,10). Jesus responded by quoting scripture and interpreting it properly. We too must be careful of those who would misinterpret scripture against the meaning intended by the Holy Spirit. One of the best ways I use to show the meaning of scripture, in addition to Church Fathers and Church Documents, is to use scripture itself to help interpret scripture.

How did Jesus teach us not to be jealous of Mary's great holiness and honor as His Mother? By pointing out that Mary's holiness and ours consists in obedience to God's word, not in a physical relationship to Christ. The Pharisees were notorious for using their physical relationship as descendants of Abraham, instead of their own obedience to God, as their means to justification (see Matt.3,John 8). Jesus saw the error of the woman in the crowd and stopped this kind of thinking immediately. This woman in the crowd is being gently spiritually chastised by Jesus, and clearly redirected in her thinking to raise her sights from the physical, to what they should be on — the spiritual. The passage in question reads:

"As he said this, a woman in the crowd raised her voice and said to him, 'Blessed is the womb that bore you, and the breasts that you sucked!' But he said, "Blessed rather are those who hear the word of God and keep it!" (Lk.11:27, 28)

Mary *is* the one who heard the word of God and kept it or obeyed it. Some misunderstand this passage as denying honor to Mary, this is a great misunderstanding of the words of Jesus. He does not deny her blessedness as His Mother, which the same gospel teaches earlier *"Blessed are you among women"* (Lk.1:42); rather, he points to what made Her Blessed. Jesus does not teach in contradiction to the Holy Spirit, there can be no contradiction between Luke 1:42 and Luke 11:27, 28. The woman does not say the same words that The Holy Spirit says through Elizabeth. They have similar words, but the phrase has a different meaning. The words of the Holy Spirit bless Mary as a person, not her body parts. Notice the difference in the words:

Luke 1:42: *Blessed are you among women, and blessed is the **fruit** of your womb.*

Luke 11:27 *Blessed is the **womb** that bore you, and the **breasts** that you sucked!*

In Luke 1:42 we see the Holy Spirit inspiring Elizabeth to proclaim Mary is blessed among women, thus blessing her person. Then we see Elizabeth blessing Jesus, the fruit of her womb, thus blessing His person. The Holy Spirit says *"Blessed are you among women"* blessing the person of Mary, not her reproductive organ or nursing organ, and *"blessed is the fruit of your womb"* which is Jesus. This second blessing is blessing Jesus, and the word "womb" is mentioned in Lk.1:42 as in Lk.11:27, but the meaning is totally different. The womb is mentioned as a connection to Mary's role as Jesus' mother, but the honor or blessing of the verse isn't the "womb" it is Jesus who is the *"fruit of your womb."*

In Luke 11:27 the blessing is directed toward the function of Mary's body through birth and nursing. It is clear from the difference in the object being blessed, that the intention is different between the woman in the crowd in Luke 11 and the Holy Spirit speaking through Elizabeth in Luke 1. The woman in the crowd is envious of Mary's role as His mother. She is discouraged because she has not been chosen for this great blessing. The woman is seeing blessedness in being His mother, whereas Jesus points out Mary's blessing was not primarily a result of being His physical mother. Mary's blessing was primarily through obedience to God's commandments, a blessing available to us all. This is so that we do not become jealous or discouraged by her great honor as His Mother. St. Augustine teaches that *"Mary was more blessed because she believed in the resurrection, than because she was His mother. Mary was more happy in having our Savior in her heart and affections, than in having conceived him in her womb."* (*The New Testament, With Catholic Commentary,* Victory Publications, P.O.Box 80636,San Marino, CA. p.99.)

Mary's true Blessing consisted of her obedience to God's word far more than by being His Mother. Mary became the Mother of God because she kept God's word, she did not keep God's word just because she was the Mother of God. Jesus teaches us this in Luke 11:28 so we do not reverse the priority. Keeping God's word is something we are called to do, as she did. And we are all called to achieve great blessings, as she did, in the same way that she did—by keeping God's commandments. Mary was the first to believe in Jesus, the first to touch Jesus, and Mary was the first Christian. She was His first believer, His first follower, and this is what her blessedness consisted of, she *"heard the Word of God and kept it".*

A simple careful study of these phrases can point out how they are not a scriptural attack by God of his own words honoring Mary as *"blessed among women"* nor denying us the chance to honor her with them. The woman is wishing she had the role of being the physical mother of Jesus, she's wishing she had a son who was so great like Jesus. An analysis of her words, and the response of Jesus to them, bears this meaning out. All we must do is remember Mary herself prophesied, *"For behold, henceforth all generations will call me blessed."* (Lk.1:48) and it was in fact the Holy Spirit that inspired St. Elizabeth, the mother of John the Baptist to honor Mary with these words in the first place! *"Elizabeth was filled with the Holy Spirit and she exclaimed with a **loud cry**, 'Blessed are you among* *women...'"* (Lk.1:41, 42)

Jesus is not going to contradict the Holy Spirit who said through St. Elizabeth *"Blessed are you among women"* and Jesus does not say: "Mary is not blessed among women"! This is the false meaning some have interpreted from this passage by not paying attention to the words.

Mary's period of testing and labor for the Lord was still under way, she had not yet taken up her position at his right hand in heaven (Mt.20:23, Rev.12:1). This woman in Luke 11:27 was not praying a Hail Mary to honor Mary in heaven as we do, especially since Mary was still on earth. And, she was not even using the same sentence we do, only some of the same words, namely "Blessed" and "womb"—with a different meaning altogether. She was speaking in a different way than the Holy Spirit did through St. Elizabeth, and this is what Jesus corrects. The woman speaks out of either a jealousy or envy of Mary's position, wishing she herself was the mother of Jesus, or out of a discouragement that she did not receive this great blessing. Either way, Jesus speaks in a way to redirect her spiritual thinking to what is best for her.

She is not his mother, nor is she going to be. Mary is the one God chose to be worthy of this unique honor; however, the reason Mary was chosen is because God knew Mary would *"hear the word of God and keep it.'* (Lk.11:28). In fact, she not only heard it, she kept it in her womb and gave birth to the word, *"And the Word was made flesh and dwelt among us."* (Jn.1:14) Mary's blessedness does not come from her physical closeness to Jesus but, through her obedience to God's word. This is the reason for her blessedness.

Jesus redirects this woman's attention from the impossible physical relationship she seeks to have with Jesus, that of being his mother, to the realistic spiritual relationship Jesus seeks to have with her, that of her being an obedient disciple. This passage speaks to us all through the centuries who might be discouraged we were not chosen for the unique privilege of the Immaculate Conception, and to be his mother. Mary's position and holiness in relation to God is overwhelming at times to us. Jesus here clarifies, in what true blessedness consists, namely union with Christ spiritually through obedience, not physically as a relative. What this woman in the crowd said was not the same as praying the word of God in Luke 1:42. It was the word of man that had some similarities, but was misdirected in its meaning. This is another reason why it is good for us to pray the word of God as our primary prayer, so that we do not speak out of our passions and weaknesses as this woman did, and have to be corrected and re-directed by God, as she was. Let us therefore pray the word of God as he wishes us to, so that we may receive the graces and blessing that he wishes to give us.

Chapter 6

The History and Promises of the Rosary

"And why is this granted me, that the mother of my Lord should come to me?" (Luke 1:43)

The History of the Rosary

After she conceived by the Holy Spirit, Mary came to visit St. Elizabeth (Lk.1:43). Now, after her Assumption into heaven, she has come to visit her children on earth (Rev.12:1,17). Throughout the centuries Mary has appeared to Christians with a message and a miracle.

Along with the miraculous healing spring in Lourdes France, and the Miracle of the Sun at Fatima, Portugal, Mary was sent by God to bring the Gospel message through a miraculous cloth to the new land. As the Catholic Church in Europe began to shrink, the Catholic Church in the Americas began to grow. Mary appeared in 1531, right as millions in Europe were abandoning the Catholic Faith for Protestantism, she came to another continent, Central America, with a miracle and a message that converted millions of Aztec Indians to Catholicism. This Miraculous Cloth of Guadalupe has many qualities which modern science has recently identified as unexplainable naturally. It is not a painting, and like the Shroud of Turin its mystical counterpart, no one quite understands how the image was made or what caused its unusual properties. This image and the message of Mary continue to bring souls to Christ through the centuries. Mary continues to bring Christ to the world, a mission given to her by God on earth, and continued in heaven.

Marian Apparitions are on solid biblical ground. Moses and Elijah appeared to Jesus *"And behold, there appeared to them Moses and Elijah."* (Mt.17:3), Jesus appeared to St. Stephen (Acts 7:55, 56) and St. Paul (Acts 9), and scripture tells us there were many apparitions of saints after the resurrection:

...the tombs were opened, and many bodies of the saints who had fallen asleep arose; and coming forth out of the tombs after his resurrection, they came into the holy city, and appeared to many. (Mt.27:52, 53)

If lesser saints such as Elijah, Moses, and others, can appear to people on earth, how much more can Mary the Mother of God! The Church allows us to believe that Mary appeared to us on earth after her Assumption. There are several Church approved apparitions (appearances) of Mary such as Guadalupe, Lourdes, and Fatima. So, the belief that Mary gave the Rosary to St. Dominic in an apparition is hardly radical. There are different paintings depicting the apparition of Mary giving the Rosary to St. Dominic. A few historians have been skeptical about it, but we also need to remember that historical record keeping over two thousand years is not to be compared with our modern methods of keeping records. Many historical records in monasteries and libraries of the past were destroyed by barbarians. The debate over how much of the Rosary evolved from inspirations of the Holy Spirit within servants of God over the centuries, and how much came from an apparition of Mary may never be settled in this world. Regardless of all the questions involved in exactly how the Rosary originated, it is certainly a prayer of great power and significance. In light of the apparitions of Lourdes and Fatima, the debate over whether Mary gave the Rosary to St. Dominic pales in relevance. The Apparitions of Lourdes and Fatima, certainly give modern historical evidence of Heaven's endorsement of this prayer. When God sends his Mother, with Rosary beads, to appear on earth with miracles, its kind of hard to ignore that evidence! Many Popes taught that the Rosary was revealed by Mary to St. Dominic. Pope Leo XIII wrote:

"The Queen of Heaven herself has given additional efficacy to this form of prayer. It was at her prompting and suggesting that the famous St. Dominic introduced and propagated this devotion as a powerful weapon against the enemies of the faith in an era that was very hostile to Catholicism, quite like our own era...Its well known origin, which famous monuments bear witness to and which we ourselves have more than once mentioned, attests to its great power...the power of the most holy rosary, the devotion which the Mother of God taught to the patriarch Dominic in order that he might propagate it." (*The Holy Rosary-Papal Teachings,* St.Paul Editions, copyright 1980 by the Daughters of St.Paul, Pgs. 72, 81)

Devotion to Mary dates back to the early Church. The oldest written prayer to the Blessed Virgin Mary dates to the year 303 A.D. This would indicate it was in common usage long before 303 A.D. This prayer was most likely a call for help by the martyrs under Diocletian:

We take refuge under the protection of your motherly mercy, O Mother of God. Despise not our fervent cries for help in the necessity in which we find ourselves. But deliver us from danger. Rescue us. Do not lead our plea into temptation, but deliver us from Danger. (Alan Schreck, *Catholic and Christian,* Servant Books, Ann Arbor, Mich. 1984, pg182.)

We see this devotion to Mary growing in strength, understanding, and depth from the early Church to the present. The Rosary is the powerful culmination of centuries of guidance and preparation by the Holy Spirit for the ultimate Marian prayer.

There are generally two theories regarding the origin of the Rosary. One is the Developmental theory and one is the Apparition theory. In my opinion, they can both be integrated in a way that has no contradiction. The use of the Our Father and Hail Mary prayer in a repetitious form was in use from the early Church, especially by monks and hermits, and developed over the centuries. Through the centuries of prayers we have gone from rocks to rosaries in our counting method. The monks moved stones on the floor to count their prayers, we use beads on a string with a cross. The union of the Mysteries with the Our Father and Hail Mary prayers, coupled with the numbering of the decades, is *the* significant development given by the apparition of the Blessed Virgin to St. Dominic. The Blessed Virgin told St. Dominic to unite the Mysteries to the prayers, and the Rosary was born. What began by the Holy Spirit in the early Church was completed by the Apparitions of Mary to the Saints.

Unfortunately, there is an ongoing debate about how much of the Apparition to St. Dominic is legend and how much is factual. Much of the argument is based on silence or a lack of evidence from other documents besides that given by Blessed Alan. Part of the issue is also the idea of the Rosary being in a state of ongoing development. The Hail Mary prayer as we know it today was shorter at the time of St.Dominic, and the number of mysteries were not as simplified as they are today. The idea of saying "Ave Maria" 150 times as part of a prayer system was used in the Eleventh Century by St. Anselm. [*The History and Devotion of the Rosary,* by Richard Gribble, C.S.C., Our Sunday Visitor Publishing Division,

Copyright 1992, pg.23/See Eadmer, The Life of St. Anselm, trans. R.W. Southern (London: Thomas Nelson and Sons, LTD,1962), pp.121-22.] This may have been part of the primary matter upon which the Rosary developed. Ultimately however, the Rosary has its foundation in the scriptures and its completion in tradition. The addition of the word *Jesus* to the end of the first part of the prayer (Lk.1:42) is possibly done by Pope Urban IV in 1261. [*The History and Devotion of the Rosary,* by Richard Gribble, C.S.C., Our Sunday Visitor Publishing Division, Copyright 1992, pg. 40/Herbert Thurston, S.J., "Hail Mary," Catholic Encyclopedia, vol.7 (New York:Robert Appleton,1910), p.111] The Council of Ephesus (431 A.D.) officially gives Mary the title of *"Theotokos"* or *"Mother of God."* This shows how Sacred Tradition and Sacred Scripture are united in the Hail Mary prayer. The last words of the Hail Mary, "Holy Mary Mother of God, pray for us sinners," can be connected to the writings of the Council of Ephesus, and later written prayers found through history. It finds its final version, the one we use, in the breviary reformed by the Council of Trent, "Holy Mary, Mother of God, pray for us sinners, now and at the hour of our death. Amen." It is important to remember that written records do not discount spoken tradition. In fact, a written record often comes after the spoken tradition or usage has been widely used and accepted. They didn't have laptop computers, copy machines, and video recorders until our century, so we can't expect their records to be like ours.

The linking of the Hail Mary prayer to the mysteries, may have been the significant contribution of St. Dominic and Our Lady's Apparition to him. Since then, Our Lady of Fatima asked for the Fatima prayer to be added at each decade, indicating still another development or new change. Also, Pope John Paul II added the option of the Mysteries of Light. So the Rosary has been in a slow state of development over the centuries. Whether there will be any more developments remains to be seen. One can argue, why didn't Mary give the ending to the Hail Mary prayer we use today if she appeared to St. Dominic? To this one might ask why didn't Our Lady give the new prayer (O my Jesus...) at Lourdes instead of waiting for Fatima? Why didn't Our Lady of Guadalupe have a Rosary in the image? Why didn't she give us the Mysteries of Light taught by Pope John Paul II? Maybe it didn't fit into heaven's timetable. Maybe God doesn't give all his gifts at once, and maybe he likes to spread them out over the centuries. We need to accept what gifts are given from heaven, make use of it as best we can, and not try to out think or second guess God.

I thought it best to include the story of the Apparition to St. Dominic for our readers, so they are free to make up their own minds. St. Louis De Montfort takes from the writings of Blessed Alan de la Roche, O.P., French Dominican Father, the origin of the Rosary. We also received the 15 Promises of the Rosary from the writings of Blessed Alan de la Roche as well. St. Louis De Montfort tells us of the origin of the Rosary:

Since the Holy Rosary is composed, principally and in substance, of the Prayer of Christ and the Angelic Salutation, that is, the Our Father and the Hail Mary, it was without doubt the first prayer and the first devotion of the faithful and has been in use all through the centuries, from the time of the apostles and disciples down to the present.

But it was only in the year 1214, however, that Holy Mother Church received the Rosary in its present form and according to the method we use today. It was given to the Church by Saint Dominic who had received it from the Blessed Virgin as a powerful means of converting the Albigensians and other sinners.

...Our Lady appeared to him, accompanied by three angels, and she said:

"Dear Dominic, do you know which weapon the Blessed Trinity wants to use to reform the world?"

"Oh, my Lady," answered Saint Dominic, "you know far better than I ..."

Then Our Lady replied:

"I want you to know that, in this kind of warfare, the battering ram has always been the Angelic Psalter which is the foundation stone of the New Testament. Therefore if you want to reach these hardened souls and win them over to God, preach my Psalter."

So he arose, comforted, and burning with zeal for the conversion of the people in that district he made straight for the Cathedral. At once unseen angels rang the bells to gather the people together and Saint Dominic began to preach.

At the very beginning of his sermon an appalling storm broke out, the earth shook, the sun was darkened, and there was so much thunder and lightning that all were very much afraid...

God wished, by means of these supernatural phenomena to so spread the new devotion of the Holy Rosary...

This miraculous way in which the devotion to the Holy Rosary was established is something of a parallel to the way in which Almighty God gave His law to the world on Mount Sinai.." (The Secret of the Rosary, by St. Louis Mary De Montfort, Montfort Publications, Bay Shore, N.Y. 11706, pgs.17-19)

Pope John Paul II wrote: "*The Rosary of the Virgin Mary, which gradually took form in the second millennium under the guidance of the Spirit of God, is a prayer loved by countless Saints and encouraged by the Magisterium...*" (Rosarium Virginis Mariae) It is clear from this that the Spirit of God guided its design, and this does not contradict St. Louis De Montfort's teaching that it is the direct work of the Holy Trinity. It is clearly designed by God. The Church Approved Apparitions at Lourdes, where Mary appeared to St. Bernadette, and at Fatima, to Blessed Francesco, Maria, and Sister Lucia, *wearing a Rosary* indicate that the Rosary is of heavenly origin and approval, being confirmed by several church approved apparitions.

Thus, we come to the source of the Fifteen Promises of Mary to Christians who pray the Rosary. According to tradition, they were given in a private revelation to St. Dominic and Blessed Alan. I list them as they have been given, along with a brief commentary of my own to help understand certain questions that may arise concerning the promises.

A Commentary on The Fifteen Promises of the Rosary

1. Whoever will faithfully serve me by the recitation of the Rosary will receive signal graces.

[A signal grace is one which helps give direction in life, especially at times when we need to make important decisions. Just as a signal light is red for stop or green for go, so too those devoted to the Rosary, will have the special guidance of Mary when they hit a crossroad in their lives. This applies to secular as well as spiritual decisions. A signal grace could range from help deciding on a job, or a spouse, to help deciding on a spiritual direction or exercise. I believe it most often involves help by signs from God on how to avoid sin, and improve or increase our prayer life.]

2. I promise my special protection and greatest graces to all those who will recite the Rosary.

[This is the second promise of Mary and it involves Mary's "special protection" and the "greatest graces." This promise alone is worth praying the Rosary for! Before Elijah is taken up to heaven in a fiery chariot, Elisha asked him, "*I pray you, let me inherit a double share of your spirit.*" (2Kgs.2) And it was granted to him, and he was a mighty prophet like Elijah. I believe in a similar way, Mary shares through God's grace, her spirit of zeal for God with her devoted ones. Hence we receive the "greatest graces" for being devoted to the Rosary. Mother Teresa spoke about her sisters praying the Rosary in the streets, in dangerous neighborhoods, and being protected from attacks. I believe many people, including myself, have escaped physical injury through Mary's intercession. Although the Rosary is a great source of physical healing and physical protection, as we saw with the stories of Father Peyton and the War and Rosary stories above, it is primarily a great source of spiritual healing and spiritual protection. It helps us deal with our guilt by giving us a divinely approved means of penance which brings us closer to Christ through meditation and it gives us new graces to protect us from temptations.]

3. The Rosary shall be a powerful armor against Hell: it shall destroy vice, decrease sin, and defeat heresies.

[This promise is to decrease sin, this does not mean eliminate or totally prevent sin. Mary will keep her promises if we do as she asks and pray the Rosary, but we must also use our free will to choose the good. As long as our will is free to choose sin, the danger we will make the wrong choice always exists. Prayer is the opposite of sin. If we persevere in prayer we will give up at least mortal sin, if not many venial sins as well. A person will either give up prayer or give up sin, the two cannot co-exist in a man's life for long.]

4. I will cause virtue and good works to flourish; it shall obtain for souls the abundant mercy of God; it shall withdraw the hearts of men from the love of the world and its vanities and shall lift them to the desire of eternal things. Oh, that souls would sanctify themselves by this means!

[As a person grows in the graces of the Rosary, Christ is formed more perfectly in their soul. Christ was the perfect example of virtue and good works, poverty and detachment. And, the Rosary will specifically help us grow in the virtue of detachment and in the 14 good works of mercy. *"Do not lay up for yourselves treasures on earth...lay up for yourselves treasures in heaven...For where your treasure is there will your heart be also."* (Mt.6:19-21) Through the graces of the Rosary, we should find ourselves less desirous and dependent on material things, and more desirous of spiritual things. The less we love the things of this world, the easier it is to part with them, and to spend less on our recreation and entertainment and more on alms for the poor and time in prayer.]

5. The soul that recommends itself to me by the meditation of the Rosary shall not perish.

[This promise emphasizes the importance of meditating on the mysteries of the Rosary, as well as praying the prayers. The meditations bind us to Christ and give us powerful graces, so that we are protected from being spiritually lost. Mary gives us yet another reason not to skip the meditations when praying the rosary.]

6. Whoever will recite the Rosary devoutly, applying himself to the consideration of its sacred mysteries, shall never be conquered by misfortune. God will not chastise him in His justice; he shall not perish by an unprovided death; if he shall be just, he shall remain in the grace of God and become worthy of eternal life.

[Again we see another reference to blessings and graces directly connected to the mysteries. The mysteries will help us deal with misfortunes. This promise does not say that a person shall never have misfortune, but that if misfortune comes it will not conquer him. The misfortune will eventually be overcome or dealt with sufficiently, provided we persevere in our Rosary and use the grace God gives us. Like a good mother, Mary will help us grow and learn through our mistakes and trials. Like children, first we learn to crawl, then to walk, then to run!]

7. Whoever will have a true devotion for the Rosary shall not die without the sacraments of the Church.

[Many times I have seen those devoted to the Rosary, stay alive long enough for the priest to come and give them the last sacraments, and sometimes that priest was me! I have anointed many who were devoted to the Rosary who were dying, and God allowed them to "hold on" until I got there. God knows the time of our death, and if we are devoted to His mother, he will bless us with the sacraments some time before our death through our regular reception, and quite likely again just before our death.]

8. Those who faithfully recite the Rosary shall have during their life and at their death the light of God and the plentitude of His graces; at the moment of death they shall participate in the merits of the saints in paradise.

[The Rosary helps us grow in the grace of God, consequently, the spiritual light of God helps us see the truths of the faith more clearly, and guides us through this life into the next.]

9. I will deliver from purgatory those who have been devoted to the Rosary.

[When we sin we receive some type of punishment or penance, (2Sam.12:13, 114 1Chr.212:8-13, 1Ptr.4:8, Jam.5:20). That penance for sins which is not completed in this life, must be completed in the next. Remember, there are sins of commission—violations of the 10 commandments, and sins of omission—neglect or violations of the 14 works of mercy or the sacraments. Devotion to the Rosary helps us avoid sins in this life. Through the Rosary our chances of going to purgatory are reduced, and if we do go our time in purgatory will be shortened.]

10. The faithful children of the Rosary shall merit a high degree of glory in heaven.

[There are different degrees of reward in heaven, (Mk.4:20, 10:35-40, Lk.19:17, 19, 1Cor.3:8, 15:41, 42, 2Cor.9:6-8, Mt.16:27). And, devotion to the Rosary is so powerful it will gain for us a closeness to God in this life, that will be fully revealed in the next.]

11. You shall obtain all that you ask of me by the recitation of the Rosary.

[Mary has great influence with her Son Jesus. Mary's request imposed upon Jesus at the wedding feast of Cana to begin his ministry of miracles. He seemed reluctant at first, but did so anyway for her sake. Had Mary not asked, they would not have received. *"When the wine failed, the mother of Jesus said to him, 'They have no wine.'...This, the first of his signs, Jesus did at Cana in Galilee, and manifested his glory; and his disciples believed in him."* (Jn.2:3,11). Now that she is in heaven she continues to intercede with her son to help us, as she helped the wedding guests at Cana. Remember there are three answers to prayer, yes, no, and please wait. St. Thomas says we receive all we ask for as long as it is part of God's plan for our salvation. There are things I asked for in the Rosary, that I thought I wanted and later learned I really didn't. Because there were things I did not know before, but later found out, making me realize my request was a mistake. I then prayed thanking God for answering those prayers with a "no". There are some things that I prayed for which took weeks, months, or years to happen, and others I still wait for. Yet, many things were answered almost instantly, when I asked for them through the Rosary. There are many things we will only get if we ask for them in prayer.]

12. All those who propagate the holy Rosary shall be aided by me in their necessities.

[If we can successfully get others to pray the Rosary, by our word or example, Mary promises to assist us in our greatest spiritual and physical needs. These "necessities" may even be unknown to us, but *"your Father knows what you need before you ask him."* (Mt.6:8) By spreading the Rosary we may bring a soul back from sin. God's word tells us, *"... whoever brings back a sinner from the error of his way will save his soul from death and will cover a multitude of sins."* (Jam.5:20)]

13. I have obtained from my divine Son that all the advocates of the Rosary shall have for intercessors the entire celestial court during their life and at the hour of their death.

[Those who advocate or promote the Rosary will have not only the prayers of Mary, the Queen of Heaven, the Queen of Angels and Saints, but the prayers of the "entire celestial court", namely all the saints in heaven, in life and at their last moments.]

14. All who recite the Rosary are my sons and brothers of my only Son, Jesus Christ.

[The Rosary helps insure our permanent membership in the family of God, when we honor the Mother of God, who is also our Spiritual Mother in heaven. It makes us like St.John the Apostle, to whom Jesus gave his mother. And, when he said these words he not only gave St. John to her, but to us as well, to be her sons and daughters. *"...standing by the cross of Jesus were his mother...When Jesus saw his mother, and the disciple whom he loved standing near, he said to his mother, "Woman, behold, your son!" Then he said to the disciple, "Behold, your mother!" And from that hour the disciple took her to his own home."* (Jn.19:25-27) With the Rosary we take her into our home on earth, and when we leave this world, she takes us into her home in heaven.]

15. Devotion to the Rosary is a great sign of predestination.

[Those who are devoted to the Rosary, bear a powerful visible sign that they are among those chosen by God. Scripture says he *"chose us in him before the foundation of the world, that we should be holy and blameless before him. He destined us in love to be his sons..."* (Eph.1:4, 5) and we, *"...have been destined and appointed to live for the praise of his glory."* (Eph.1:12) The mystery of free will and grace will be understood only in the next life, for Jesus said: *"You did not choose me, but I chose you and appointed you..."* (Jn.15:16) On predestination the Catechism of the Catholic Church says:

CCC(600) "To God, all moments of time are present in their immediacy. When therefore he establishes his eternal plan of "predestination", he includes in it each person's free response to his grace: *'In this city, in fact, both Herod and Pontius Pilate, with the Gentiles and the peoples of Israel, gathered together against your holy servant Jesus, whom you anointed, to do whatever your hand and your plan had predestined to take place.'* For the sake of accomplishing his plan of salvation, God permitted the acts that flowed from their blindness."

CCC(2012): "We know that in everything God works for

good with those who love him... For those whom he foreknew he also predestined to be conformed to the image of his son, in order that he might be the first-born among many brethren. And those whom he predestined he also called; and those whom he called he also justified; and those whom he justified he also glorified." (Rom.8:28-30)

(Imprimatur for 15 Promises was given by Patrick J.Hayes, D.D., Archbishop of New York)

Final Exhortation to Pray the Rosary

Mary gave these promises to man hundreds of years ago, and they are still valid today. Mary promises many wonderful things to those who embrace devotion to the Rosary.

Through the Rosary the life of Christ becomes your life, and Christ lives within you. In praying the Rosary the power of God becomes manifest in your soul, so that your mind and heart are open to the mind and heart of God. Then, you see life and the world as God does. You see the good and the evil in the world, and can see what you need to change in your life to become more Christlike.

The message of the Rosary is the message of the Gospel. The Rosary is true evangelization, it contains the story of Christ, the worship of Christ, and the honor of Mary. The Rosary contains the wisdom of Christianity. It has within itself the life of Christ from his conception to his Ascension, the life of Mary from her consent to be the Mother of God to her Son Crowning her in Heaven.

The power of the Rosary is the power of Christ. Reading scripture is important, and going to mass is essential. However, it is through the word of God in action, through prayer, especially through the Gospel prayer of the Rosary, that God helps us grow in the love of these. The Rosary gives the wisdom of the Holy Spirit and helps you to hear God talking to you in scripture, as well as grow in your ability to see God hidden in the Eucharist. The Rosary helps us understand scripture, and the sacraments more fully. I pray:

A Prayer For God's Word

God grant us your Word,
Grant that I may hear the Word of God in scripture,
God grant that I may pray the Word of God in the Rosary,
God grant that I may receive the Word of God in Holy Communion,
God grant that I may live through your Word,
proclaim your Word,
and be one with your Word
- In this life and in eternal life. Amen.

As we saw in Father Peyton, through the Rosary, a man can make his life a living miracle of God's love. His life can be transformed from sorrow to joy, weakness to strength, confusion to order, unrest to peace, fallen nature to the risen nature, from sin to grace, from being lost in the dangers of the world to being found in the safety of God, from being dependent on the pleasures of sense to being free in the happiness of the Spirit, and from the search for God to the possession of God. All these are given in return to a man who gives his soul to God, more and more, day by day, through the Rosary.

The miracle of the Rosary is its power to transform our lives from being servants of the world into saints of God. From generation to generation the Rosary is a devotion which never dies, but is always being born again in each new soul that discovers its power. The Rosary gives us aid in knowing and loving God , in keeping his commandments, in detachment, and virtue.

People can experience a miracle in their lives through the daily Rosary. They can experience a living faith which gives a new understanding of life, a new peace of knowing and loving God, and a new power to overcome their weaknesses and solve the problems of their lives.

Through the Rosary a desire to know, love, and serve God supplants the desire to know, love, and serve the world. Through the Rosary you will not only be happier now in this world than those who have the world, but you will have the hope and promise of eternal life.

The Rosary is the life of Christ, the Gospel brought to life in your heart, soul, and mind. The Rosary has a unique relationship to scripture, different from all other scriptural prayer. It is the most fully Gospel prayer since it contains the two most powerful prayers of the New Testament, and meditations of the life, death, and resurrection of Christ—which is the Gospel itself.

The prayer of the Rosary should not be called by some Christians a thing which takes honor away from God, since it causes us to grow in the love of God and in the observance of His commandments. Scripture says:

> You will know them by their fruits. Are grapes gathered from thorns, or figs from thistles? So, every sound tree bears good fruit, but the bad tree bears evil fruit. A sound tree cannot bear evil fruit, nor can a bad tree bear good fruit. Every tree that does not bear good fruit is cut down and thrown into the fire. Thus you will know them by their fruits. (Mt.7:16-20)

The fruits of the Rosary are the Twelve Fruits of the Holy Spirit:

1. Charity
2. Joy
3. Peace
4. Patience
5. Kindness
6. Goodness
7. Long-suffering
8. Humility
9. Fidelity
10. Modesty
11. Continence
12. Chastity
(Gal.5:22, 23, 24)

The Rosary bears the fruits of increased love of God and detachment from the world, increased grace and decreased sin. It cannot be a bad tree with these results. Can a bad spiritual tree help someone keep the commandments of Christ? No, as our Lord has said, only a good tree bears good fruit, and the Rosary bears good fruit.

If the Rosary took honor away from God by giving honor to Mary it could not advance people in living the teachings of Christ. In view of the good effects the Rosary has had on so many Christians, it is not reasonable that some Christians should deny its legitimacy as a fully

Christian prayer.

In the Rosary we give Mary the same honor that God the Father commanded the Archangel Gabriel to give her in the Gospel (Lk.1:27,42). The Gospel itself begins with the Honor of Mary, and She is the way chosen by God to enter the world. Mary is the chosen one of God, the one He chose to be His mother and our Mother. Those who don't like Mary in their spiritual life, don't like the choice of God! It was He who chose to put her in a role that is central to the Gospel, and give her a role in salvation that continues in heaven through her prayers for her spiritual children. Those who have Christ in their soul, have Mary as their spiritual Mother. The more they realize this, the more they will grow.

God is there any time you want him. It is up to you to accept him, to pray, and receive his life. He will manifest and reveal himself to you in prayer. It is up to you to pray and behold the face of God. It is up to you to use the advantage of devotion to Mary in the Rosary, to accelerate your spiritual growth. It is hard to grow up in life with only a father, a mother makes so many things in life so much easier. Mary is the spiritual mother that many of us never knew we had. She is anxious to help us and show us her love, the love she has received from God. If we pray the Rosary, Mary can do wonderful things for us.

I am not saying you will eliminate all problems and all sins in life if you pray the Rosary. No, you will still have the cross, you will still have weaknesses, problems and sins. However, instead of being slaughtered by life's problems and not knowing the best way to deal with them, you will now have a decent weapon on the spiritual battlefield of life. A good soldier can get far with a good weapon, so too can the spiritual soldier get far if he prays the Rosary well. The Rosary is the new advanced spiritual weapon from heaven, it is the weapon of the new covenant of Jesus Christ.

If people are stupid enough to stop praying, the devil is smart enough to know he has a window of opportunity to exploit and do all he can to make sure they don't return to prayer. He may offer a new sin opportunity to distract them, he may get thoughts into their head like, "praying didn't really do any good. It didn't help me, why should I bother taking the time and effort to do it. I'll do something else, God still loves me....."

There were some times in life when I very foolishly, under faulty reasoning, abandoned praying the Rosary. At the very least I lost peace of soul, and at the very worst I lapsed into sins that should have never been. But I still hope in God's words of loving forgiveness, and I can make the contrition of King David and others in scripture my own:

*"If thou, O Lord, shouldst mark iniquities, Lord, who could stand?
But there is forgiveness with thee... "* (Ps.130:3,4)

"For a righteous man falls seven times, and rises again..."(Prv.24:16)

"God, be merciful to me a sinner!"(Lk.18:13)

*"O Lord, rebuke me not in thy anger, nor chasten me in thy wrath!
For thy arrows have sunk into me, and thy hand has come down on me...
For my iniquities have gone over my head; they weigh like a burden too
heavy for me...
My wounds grow foul and fester because of my foolishness, I am utterly
bowed down and prostrate; all the day I go about in mourning...
For I pray, 'Only let them not rejoice over me, who boast against me when
my foot slips!'...
I confess my iniquity, I am sorry for me sin..."* (Ps.38:1, 2, 4, 6, 16, 18)

*"Have mercy on me, O God, according to thy steadfast love;
according to thy abundant mercy blot out my transgressions.
Wash me thoroughly from my iniquity, and cleanse me from my sin!
For I know my transgressions, and my sin is ever before me.
Against thee, thee only, have I sinned, and done that which is evil in
thy sight, so that thou art justified in thy sentence and blameless in thy
judgment...
Create in me a clean heart, O God, and put a new and right spirit within
me.
Cast me not away from thy presence, and take not thy Holy Spirit from
me.
Restore to me the joy of thy salvation...then I will teach transgressors thy
ways and sinners will return to thee."* (Ps.51:1-4, 10-13)

*"I knew that thou art a gracious God and merciful, slow to anger, and
abounding in steadfast love..."* (Jon.4:2)

Whatever mountains of guilt I feel for my past failures and whatever
temptations to despair I may feel in consequence of sins, I still know God

is all powerful and can forgive and fix my mistakes. I turn to the God who writes straight with crooked lines, the God who turns sinners into saints. I know that if I make it to heaven, whatever bothers me now will be gone forever and God will *"wipe away every tear from their eyes, and death shall be no more, neither shall there be mourning nor crying nor pain any more for the former things have passed away."* (Rev.21:4)

In heaven there will be no more guilt, but complete forgiveness forever and ever:

"For the accuser of our brethren has been thrown down, who accuses them day and night before our God." (Rev.12:10)

God brings good out of evil, and I know that although the times in my life I have abandoned prayer were evil, I learned to appreciate prayer all the more when I returned to it. If I learned anything good from turning away from the Rosary, it was not to turn away from the Rosary.

"We know that in everything God works for good with those who love him, who are called according to his purpose.." (Rom.8:28) In his commentary on this passage, St. Augustine adds, "even sin". In "everything God works for good", so even our sins can be a way for us to grow if we can learn from them how to avoid more sins in the future.

The Rosary is an ancient Christian prayer that is as alive in the 21st century as it was centuries ago. It has the power to bring God into our lives, and apply His power and wisdom to our weaknesses and problems. If you are looking for a sure way to know and experience his love — **The Rosary is the Answer.**

Poem: Little Man with the Rosary

These are some of my personal reflections on the wisdom, the power, and the secret of the Rosary in a poetic format:

Little Man with the Rosary

"Fear not, little flock, for it is your Father's good pleasure to give you the kingdom. Sell your possessions, and give alms; provide yourselves with purses that do not grow old, with a treasure in the heavens that does not fail, where no thief approaches and no moth destroys. For where your treasure is, there will your heart be also." (Lk.12:32-34)

Little man, the Rosary is a treasure from God.
Take this gift from heaven
and let it lift you to heaven.
Pick up the Rosary and lift your soul to the Lord.
Pick up the Rosary and pray to God with Mary,
Join her prayers in heaven to your prayers on earth,
and God's will is done on earth as it is in heaven (Mt.6:10).
Pick up the Rosary and change your life forever.

Little man with a choice to make,
do you see the key to the kingdom of God
in your hands, when you hold a Rosary?
Do you see in your hand the power to change the world?
-The power to change *your* world?

Little man standing on the earth, beware of this world!
It wants to take your love from God (1Jn.2:15-17).
The world will tell you there is no life,
no power, and no point in prayer
-Because the world follows the way of the fool (Ps.53:1),
It is blinded by the flesh to the wisdom of the Spirit.
It chooses the ways of the animals over the ways of the angels.
It's reason is passion and its logic is madness,
-the madness that would lose an eternal soul
for a moment of pleasure.
This is a proud worldly wisdom
whose terms are a dictionary of lies (Jn.8:44),
and whose map leads to death (Mt.7:13).

Little Man with a humble heart,
Open the book of truth
and embrace the life which leads to freedom

Discover the truth of the Gospel by living it.
Know for sure its house is founded upon spiritual rock.
(Mt.5:7:25/16:18).

Little man with a big heart,
know as truth from God that
If a man chooses the life of sin over the life of prayer,
He has lost his fortune in the spirit to the house of the flesh
- a house destined for destruction (Mt.7:27).
Do not allow yourself to be sold (Mt.27:5) into this parade of injustice.
Realize you potential is infinite,
your chance to choose Divine.

Little man with your Rosary beads,
do not let your opponent who is armed with a reed (Mk.15:19), take your
sword from your hand.
Little man with the Rosary beads no one can match your strength
For the power of the creator of all things is at your command
The power of your opponents is in your hand (Mt.26:53/Jn.19:11)
Little man with your Rosary beads do you know the power is within your
hands to shake the earth? (Mk.11:23, 24)

Little man with your little Rosary,
Do you know it is within your power through simple prayer and meditation
to straighten the arch of sin and receive power, honor, and glory
A thousand times above and beyond that of the earth?
(Lk.4:6-8, Jn.18:36)
Do you know that you can rise to an estate in the city of God (Jn.14:2)
and possess it forever without fear of loss? (Mt.6:20, 21 /Rev.21:4)
- unlike the estates of this world (Mt.6:19)
which pass on the night of death and judgment (Lk.12:20).

Little man holding the Rosary beads
do you know that
to accept the loss of your life in this world (Mt.10:39)
you inherit the reign of a kingdom
More mighty than the universe (Mt.24:29),
More brilliant that the sun (Rev.21:23),

The Rosary is the Answer

More powerful than all the armies that ever fought (Rev.19:11-15),
More beautiful than all the women who ever lived (Rev.21:2),
More precious than all the diamonds, pearls (Rev.18:12, 16) and gold that ever existed?

Little man with your Rosary beads do you know what a treasure you have? (Mt.13:45)

Little man do you know how big you really are?
Do you know you sit upon a goldmine when you own a soul (Mt.13:44),
And your Rosary is the tool that can dig out your hidden treasure?

Little man with the Rosary,
Do not accept defeat
when you can conquer your enemy(Rev.3:5,21),
-By the acceptance of suffering in this life (Lk.23:41)
and the will to persevere in prayer,
you are given an exit to paradise *(Lk.23:43)*
A road to the house of peace (Is.35:8).

Little man with the Rosary in your hands,
You are little in the eyes of the world,
But you are great in the eyes of God (1Sam.16:7)
-In silent prayer you move the world
(Mt.6:6, Jas.5:16-18).

"In these days he went out into the hills to pray; and all night he continued in prayer to God." (Lk.6:12)

Chapter 7

How to Pray the Rosary

"Hail, full of grace, the Lord is with you!.... Blessed are you among women, and blessed is the fruit of your womb!
...For behold, henceforth all generations will call me blessed."
(Luke 1:28, 42, 48)

Nine simple steps to Praying the Rosary:

1. Make the Sign of the Cross.
2. Pray the Apostles' Creed on the crucifix.
3. Pray the Lord's prayer on the first bead.
4. Pray the Hail Mary prayer on the next three beads. (The three beads are a symbol for the Trinity).
5. Pray the Glory Be, and announce the first mystery for meditation. (Mysteries are listed below.)
6. Pray the Lord's prayer on the next bead.
7. Pray ten Hail Marys on the next ten beads while meditating on the mystery.
8. Repeat steps 5-7 again on each remaining decade. (Decade meaning the Our Father, ten Hail Marys, and the Glory be, with the mystery.)
9. End by praying the Hail Holy Queen.

The Mysteries of the Rosary

The Joyful Mysteries:
(Usually said on Monday and Thursday.)

1. The Annunciation (Lk.1:28-For Humility)
2. The Visitation (Lk.1:41-42-For Love of Neighbor)
3. The Nativity (Lk.2:7-For Poverty)
4. The Presentation (Lk.2:22-23-For Obedience)
5. The Finding in the Temple (Lk.2:46-For Joy in Finding Jesus)

The Luminous Mysteries:
(Usually said on Thursdays)

6. The Baptism of Jesus (Matt.3:16-17- For Openness to the Holy Spirit)
7. The Wedding at Cana (Jn. 2:5-7-To Jesus Through Mary)
8. Proclaiming the Kingdom (Matt. 10:7-8-Repentance and Trust in God)
9. The Transfiguration (Luke 9:29-35- Desire for Holiness)
10. The Institution of the Eucharist (Luke 22:19-20-Adoration)

The Sorrowful Mysteries:
(Usually said on Tuesday and Friday)

11. The Agony in the Garden (Lk.22:44-45-For sorrow for sin)
12. The Scourging at the Pillar (Jn.19:1-For purity)
13. The Crowning with Thorns (Mt.27:28-29-For courage)
14. The Carrying of the Cross (Jn.19:17-For Patience)
15. The Crucifixion (Lk.23:46-For Perseverance)

The Glorious Mysteries:
(Usually said on Wednesday, Saturday, and Sunday)

16. The Resurrection (Mk.16:6-For Faith)
17. The Ascension (Mk.16:19-For Hope)
18. The Descent of the Holy Spirit (Acts2:4-For Love of God)
19. The Assumption of Mary (Rev.12:1-For a happy death)
20. The Coronation of Mary (Rev.12:1-For trust in Mary's Intercession)

The Prayers of the Rosary:

The Sign of the Cross

In the name of the Father, and of the Son, and of the Holy Spirit. Amen. (Jn.14:14, Mt.28:19)

The Apostle's Creed

I believe in God the Father Almighty, Creator of heaven and earth; and in Jesus Christ, His only Son, Our Lord; Who was conceived by the Holy Spirit, born of the Virgin Mary, suffered under Pontius Pilate, was crucified, died, and was buried. He descended into hell; on the third day He arose again from the dead. He ascended into heaven, and is seated at the right hand of the Father. He will come again to judge the living and the dead. I believe in the Holy Spirit, the Holy Catholic Church, the communion of saints, the forgiveness of sins, the resurrection of the body, and life everlasting. Amen.

The Hail Mary

Hail Mary, full of grace! The Lord is with thee. Blessed art thou among women, and blessed is the fruit of thy womb, Jesus. Holy Mary Mother of God, pray for us sinners, now and at the hour of our death. Amen.
(Based on Luke 1:28, 42 and Tradition)

The Lord's Prayer

Our Father who art in heaven, hallowed be Thy name. Thy kingdom come, Thy will be done on earth, as it is in heaven. Give us this day our daily bread. And forgive us our trespasses as we forgive those who trespass against us. And lead us not into temptation, but deliver us from evil. Amen
(Matthew 6:9-13)

The Glory Be

Glory be to the Father, and to the Son, and to the Holy Spirit. As it was in the beginning, is now, and ever shall be, world without end. Amen.
(Based on Matthew 28:19 and Tradition)

Hail Holy Queen

Hail Holy Queen, Mother of Mercy, our life our sweetness and our hope. To Thee do we cry, poor banished children of Eve. To Thee do we send up our sighs, mourning and weeping in this valley of tears. Turn then, most gracious advocate thine eyes of mercy towards us, and after this our exile, show unto us the blessed fruit of Thy womb, Jesus. O clement, O loving, O sweet virgin Mary.

The Fatima Prayer:

O my Jesus, forgive us our sins, save us from the fires of hell, lead all souls to heaven, especially those in most need of thy mercy. (This prayer was given in a private apparition by Our Lady of Fatima who requested it be added to the Rosary after each "Glory Be".)